AIKIDO

The Co-ordination of Mind and Body for Self-defense

by

Koichi Tohei

Souvenir Press
London

合氣道

Editor

Morihei Uyeshiba

Originator of AIKIDO

———◆———

Author

Koichi Tohei

The Chief Instructor at AIKIDO Headquarters

© 1961 by Rikugei Publishing House
All rights reserved
First published by
Rikugei Publishing House, Japan
First published in Great Britain 1966
by Souvenir Press Ltd.,
95 Mortimer Street, London W1N 8HP

Reprinted 1975
Reprinted 1982
Reprinted 1986

No part may be reproduced in any
form without permission in writing
from the publisher except by a
reviewer who wishes to quote brief
passages for the purpose of a review.

Printed in Great Britain by
Fletcher & Son Ltd, Norwich and bound by
Richard Clay (The Chaucer Press) Ltd
Bungay, Suffolk

Prof. Morihei Uyeshiba
Originator of AIKIDO

Kisshomaru Uyeshiba

The Director of the General Headquarters Arena of AIKIDO.

Professor Uyeshiba (right) and the author. (1953)

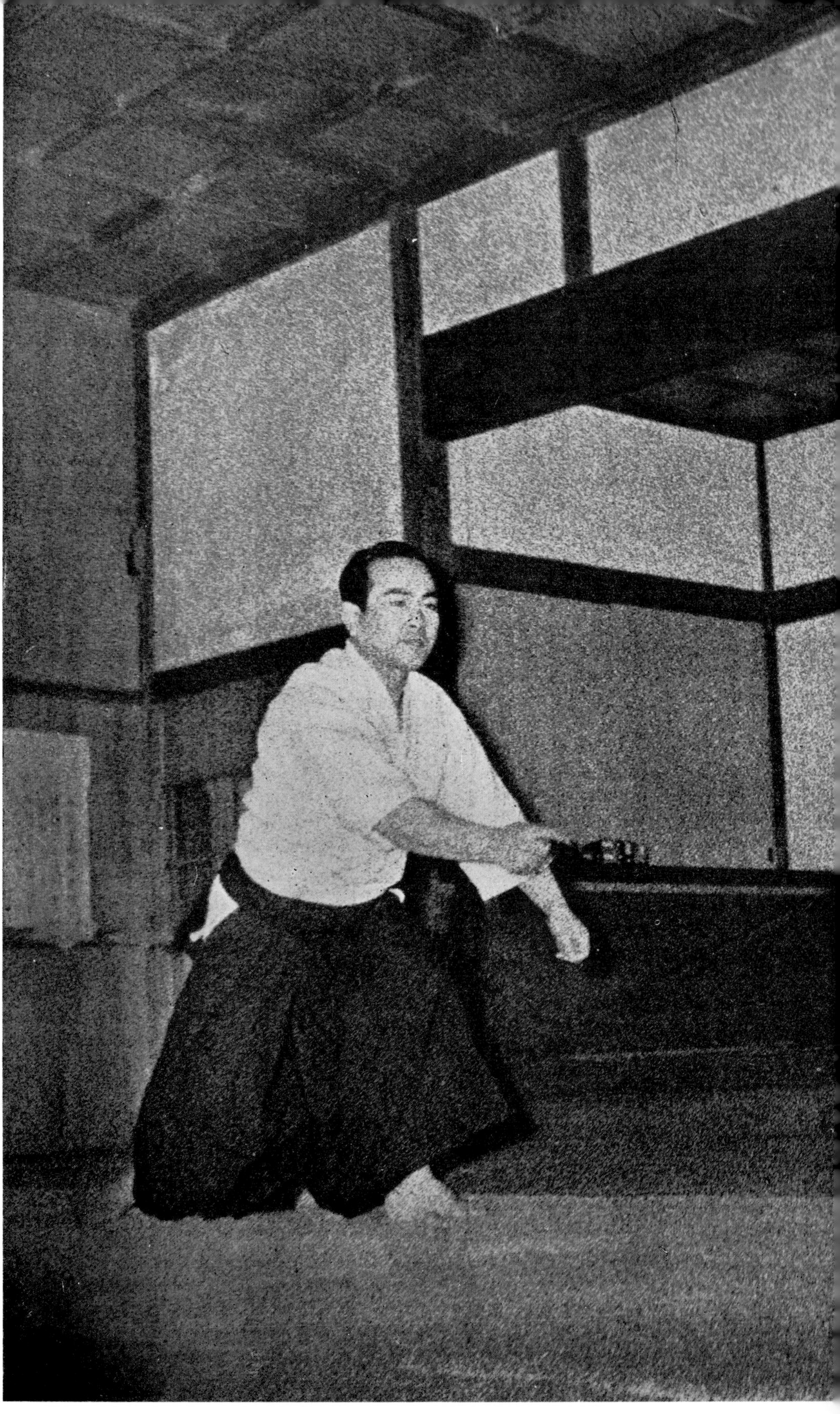

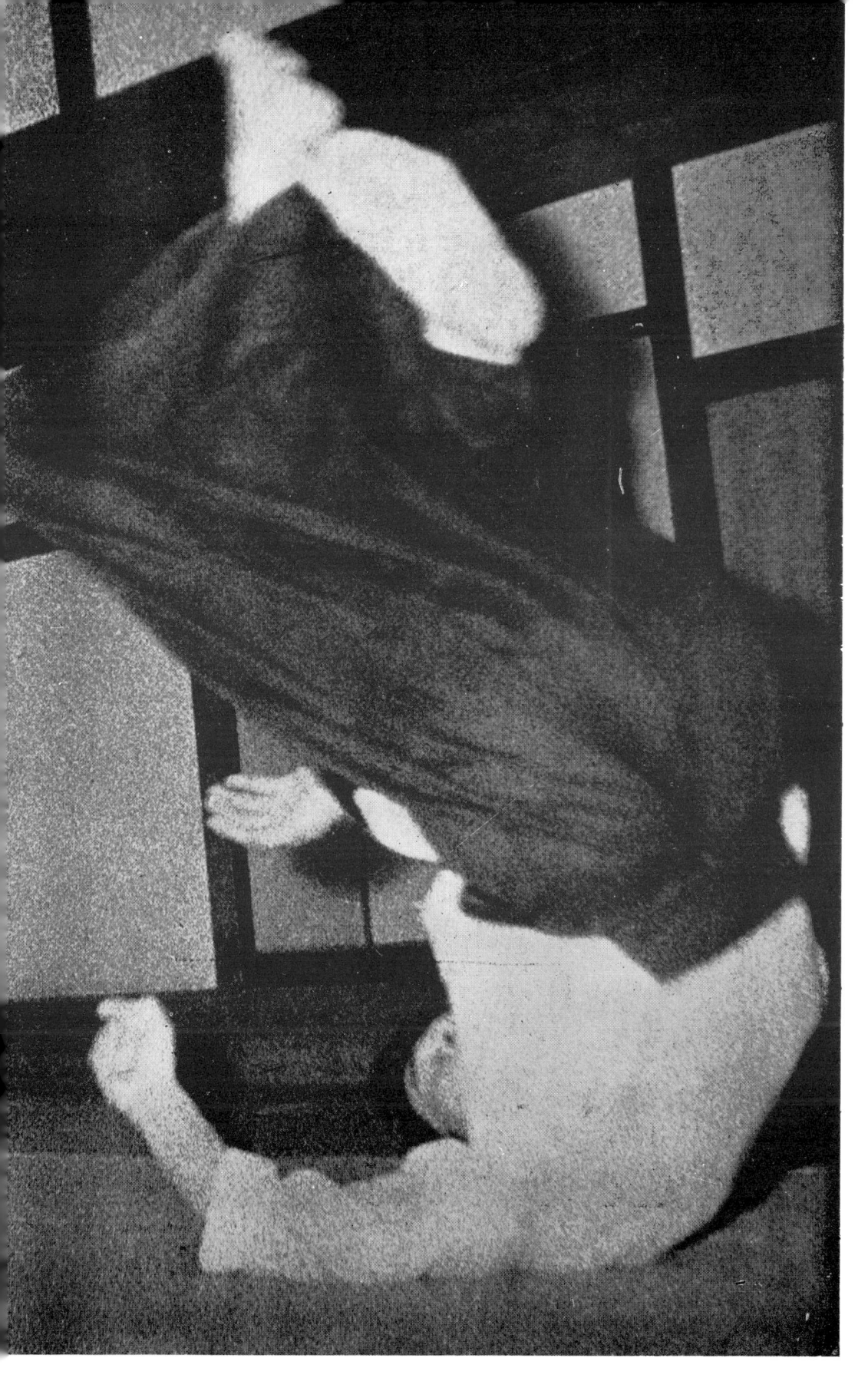

KATATE-TORI RYOTE-MOCHI KOKYU-NAGE

The Author, Koichi Tohei

No sooner does Prof. Uyeshiba reach AIKIDO Headquarters than he begins to give lessons to instructors and trainees, almost without taking time to change his clothes.

KATATE-TORI KOKYU-NA

Demonstrations by Professor Uyeshiba himself.

Training in an art to overcome others by the motion of the body only without using hands.

Performance of Professor Uyeshiba as he gives lessons.

KATATE-TORI RYOTE-MOCHI KOKYU-NAGE

All instructors AIKIDO Headquarters.

Instructors' training at AIKIDO Headquarters.

Many older trainees in morning lesson.

Women trainees in action among men trainees.

Women trainees in action.

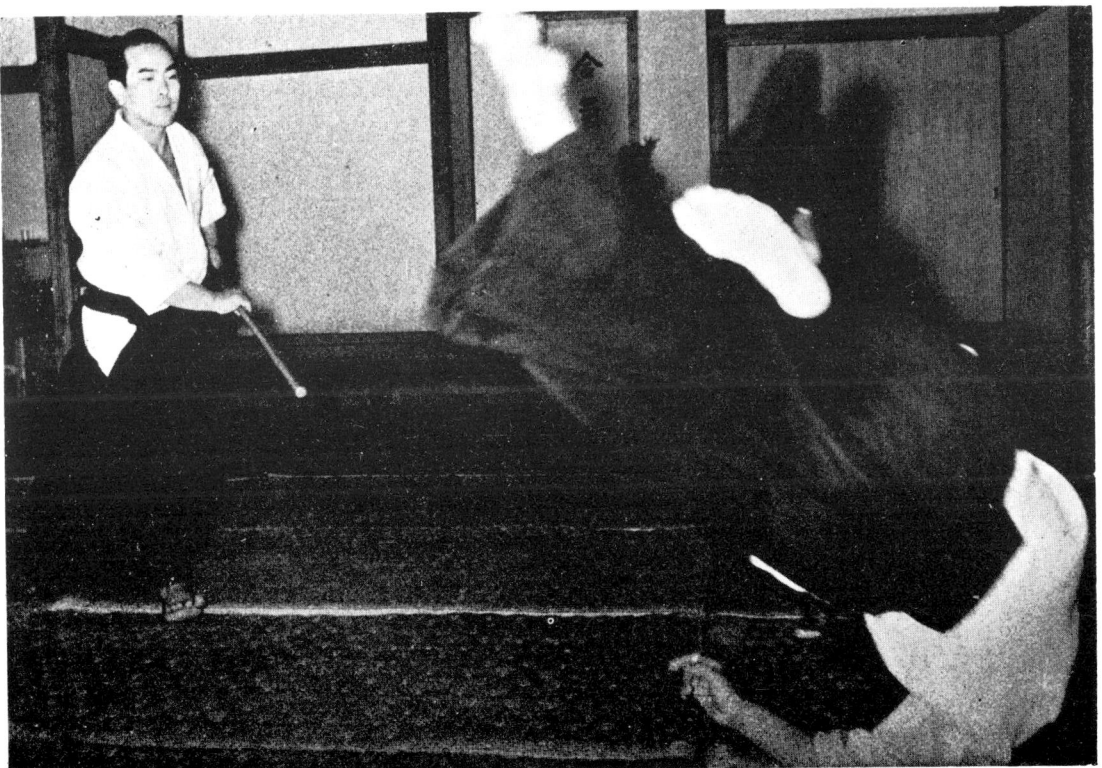

Throwing an opponent with a club, after taking his weapon away instantaneously.

The author overwhelms a man twice as big as he is.

The author as Honorary Captain of Hawaii Police Force.

The General Headquarters Arena of AIKIDO
102 Wakamatsu-cho, Shinjuku-ku
TOKYO, JAPAN

FOREWORD

The originator and revered founder of *AIKIDO* is Morihei Uyeshiba. So revolutionary were the principles he propounded that there was an insistent public demand for a book explaining the new art, and there were attempts to satisfy this demand by pamphleteers who had at best only a shallow knowledge of the subject. It was not until permission was granted by the founder to his son, Kisshomaru Uyeshiba, to publish "*AIKIDO*" that the demand was adequately met in August 1957. The author of this book is the director of the general headquarters arena of *AIKIDO*, at 102 Wakamatsu-cho, Shinjuku-ku, Tokyo, Japan.

Because the book contains a record of Professor Uyeshiba's own experiences in developing *AIKIDO* as well as an exposition of the ideals and practical application of the art and a detailed explanation of every hold, "*AIKIDO*" was warmly received by all practitioners of the art.

Now that *AIKIDO* has spread from Japan to America, France, Italy, Hawaii and other parts of the earth, the fact that this book is published only in Japanese and has not yet been translated into English to make the knowledge of *AIKIDO* available to a larger public is one cause for dissatisfaction.

It must be acknowledged that the thought processes of the Japanese and the sentence structure of the Japanese language make translation a difficult task, and it is equally difficult to present the spiritual overtones and undertones of *AIKIDO* so that non-Japanese may hear them clearly.

I am making this attempt to introduce *AIKIDO* in English only because I have learned from the trips I made to Hawaii and the United States mainland about conditions that exist there and know from teaching several thousand students that there is among them an ardent desire to have a book of this kind to study.

Professor Uyeshiba has given me his kind permission to proceed and I offer "*AIKIDO*" in the hope that it will be a good companion to fellow practitioners and a guide to those who wish to pursue the study of this art.

Koichi Tohei

CONTENTS

Chapter I. INTRODUCTION 31
    AIKIDO AND NATURE 33
    THE SPIRIT OF LOVING PROTECTION FOR ALL NATURE 34
    THE RATIONALE OF NON-RESISTANCE 35

Chapter II. *AIKIDO* AND MENTAL AND PHYSICAL
    COORDINATION 37
    COORDINATION OF MIND AND BODY 39
    RELATION BETWEEN MIND AND BODY 41
    TRAINING OF MIND AND BODY 42
    SEIKA-NO-ITTEN (THE ONE POINT) 46

Chapter III. PROFESSOR *MORIHEI UYESHIBA* 49

Chapter IV. THE ARTS OF *AIKIDO* 55
    ATTITUDE TOWARD TRAINING 57
      1. Continue To Practice Earnestly 57
      2. Have A Receptive, Open-Minded Attitude 58
      3. Rules During Practice 58
    AIKI TAISO (*AIKI* EXERCISES) 59
      1. NIKYO 59
      2. KOTE-GAESHI 60
      3. Relax 61
      4. "Rowing" Exercise 61
      5. SHOMEN-UCHI IKKYO 62
      6. ZENGO UNDO 63
      7. HAPPO UNDO 64
      8. KOKYU-HO UNDO 65
      9-1. TEKUBI KOSA UNDO 67
      9-2. TEKUBI JOHO KOSA UNDO 68
      10. SAYU UNDO 69
      11. UDE FURI UNDO 71

12.	USHIRO TORI UNDO	73
13.	USHIRO TEKUBI TORI ZENSHIN UNDO	73
14.	USHIRO TEKUBI TORI KOTAI UNDO	75
15.	KOHO TENTO (KOHO UKEMI) UNDO	75
16.	ZEMPO KAITEN (ZEMPO UKEMI) UNDO	77

EXPLANATION OF THE REAL ARTS OF *AIKIDO* 79

1. Fifty Arts 79
2. The Words Most Frequently Used in AIKIDO 82
   - A. KI 82
   - B. KOKYU 84
   - C. HANMI 84
   - D. MA-AI 84
   - E. ORENAI-TE (Unbendable Arm) 85
   - F. FUDO NO SHISEI 85
   - G. IRIMI 85
   - H. TENKAN 85
   - I. NAGE 85
   - J. UKE 85

EXPLANATION OF ARTS OR TECHNIQUES 86

No. 1.	KATATE-TORI KOKYU-HO TENKAN	86
No. 2.	KATATE-TORI KOKYU-HO IRIMI	88
No. 3.	KATATE-TORI KOKYU-NAGE (Opposite Side)	89
No. 4.	KATATE-TORI KOTE-GAESHI (Opposite Side)	92
No. 5.	KOKYU-DOSA	94
No. 6.	KATATE-TORI KOKYU-NAGE	96
No. 7.	KATATE-TORI KOTE-GAESHI	98
No. 8.	KATATE-TORI KOKYU-NAGE IRIMI	99
No. 9.	KATATE-TORI KOKYU-NAGE TENKAN	100
No. 10.	KATATE-TORI KOKYU-NAGE TENKAN (KATATE-TORI KAITEN-NAGE)	102
No. 11.	KATA-TORI IKKYO IRIMI	103
No. 12.	KATA-TORI IKKYO TENKAN	106

No. 13.	KATA-TORI NIKYO IRIMI	107
No. 14.	KATA-TORI NIKYO TENKAN	108
No. 15.	KATA-TORI KOKYU-NAGE IRIMI	108
No. 16.	KATA-TORI KOKYU-NAGE TENKAN	109
No. 17.	YOKOMEN-UCHI SHIHO-NAGE	110
No. 18.	YOKOMEN-UCHI KOKYU-NAGE TENKAN (A)	113
No. 19.	YOKOMEN-UCHI KOKYU-NAGE TENKAN (B)	114
No. 20.	YOKOMEN-UCHI KOKYU-NAGE TENKAN (C)	115
No. 21.	YOKOMEN-UCHI KOKYU-NAGE IRIMI (A)	116
No. 22.	YOKOMEN-UCHI KOKYU-NAGE IRIMI (B)	117
No. 23.	SHOMEN-UCHI KOKYU-NAGE IRIMI	117
No. 24.	SHOMEN-UCHI KOTE-GAESHI	119
No. 25.	SHOMEN-UCHI IKKYO IRIMI	119
No. 26.	SHOMEN-UCHI IKKYO TENKAN	121
No. 27.	SHOMEN-UCHI NIKYO IRIMI	121
No. 28.	SHOMEN-UCHI NIKYO TENKAN	121
No. 29.	SHNMEN-UCHI SANKYO IRIMI	121
No. 30.	SHOMEN-UCHI SANKYO TENKAN	123
No. 31.	MUNE-TSUKI KOTE-GAESHI	123
No. 32.	MUNE-TSUKI KAITEN-NAGE	125
No. 33.	MUNE-TSUKI HANTAI TENKAN	126
No. 34.	MUNE-TSUKI KOTE-GAESHI HANTAI TENKAN	127
No. 35.	KATATE-TORI RYOTE-MOCHI KOKYU-NAGE IRIMI	127
No. 36.	KATATE-TORI RYOTE-MOCHI KOKYU-NAGE TENKAN (A)	129
No. 37.	KATATE-TORI RYOTE-MOCHI KOKYU-NAGE TENKAN (B)	132
No. 38.	KATATE-TORI RYOTE-MOCHI KOTE-GAESHI	132
No. 39-1.	KATATE-TORI RYOTE-MOCHI NIKYO (A)	133
No. 39-2.	KATATE-TORI RYOTE-MOCHI NIKYO (B)	133
No. 40.	USHIRO TEKUBI-TORI IKKYO	134
No. 41.	USHIRO TEKUBI-TORI KOTE-GAESHI	136
No. 42.	USHIRO TEKUBI-TORI SANKYO	137
No. 43.	USHIRO TEKUBI-TORI KOTE-GAESHI TENKAN	137
No. 44.	USHIRO HIJI-TORI KOTE-GAESHI	138

    No. 45. USHIRO KATA-TORI KOTE-GAESHI 139
    No. 46-1. USHIRO KATA-TORI KOKYU-NAGE (AGO-TSUKI-AGE) 139
    No. 46-2. USHIRO KATA-TORI KOKYU-NAGE 140
    No. 47. USHIRO KUBI-SHIME KOKYU-NAGE 141
    No. 48. USHIRO-TORI KOKYU-NAGE 143
    No. 49. USHIRO KATATE-TORI KUBI-SHIME SANKYO (A) 145
    No. 50. USHIRO KATATE-TORI KUBI-SHIME SANKYO (B) 146
  CONCLUSION 148
Chapter V. *AIKIDO* AS A WAY TO MAINTAIN HEALTH 151
  MENTAL CONSIDERATION 153
    1. Exaltation Of Life Force 153
    2. Positive Use Of Mind..................................... 154
  PHYSICAL CONSIDERATION 155
    1. Exercising The Entire Body 155
    2. Exercises To Make The Body Soft 156
    3. Avoid Doing Unreasonable Things 157
Chapter VI. *AIKIDO* AS THE ARTS OF SELF-DEFENSE 159
  MENTAL CONSIDERATION 161
    1. The Sixth Sense 161
    2. Immovable Mind 162
  PHYSICAL CONSIDERATION 163
    1. Practice Adapted To Real Fighting........................ 163
    2. Not To Struggle Against Your Opponent's Power 164
    3. An Instance Of Taking A Pistol Away 164
  SELF-DEFENSE IN ITS DEEPER MEANING 168
Chapter VII. A SKETCH OF THE AUTHOR'S LIFE 171

CHAPTER I
INTRODUCTION

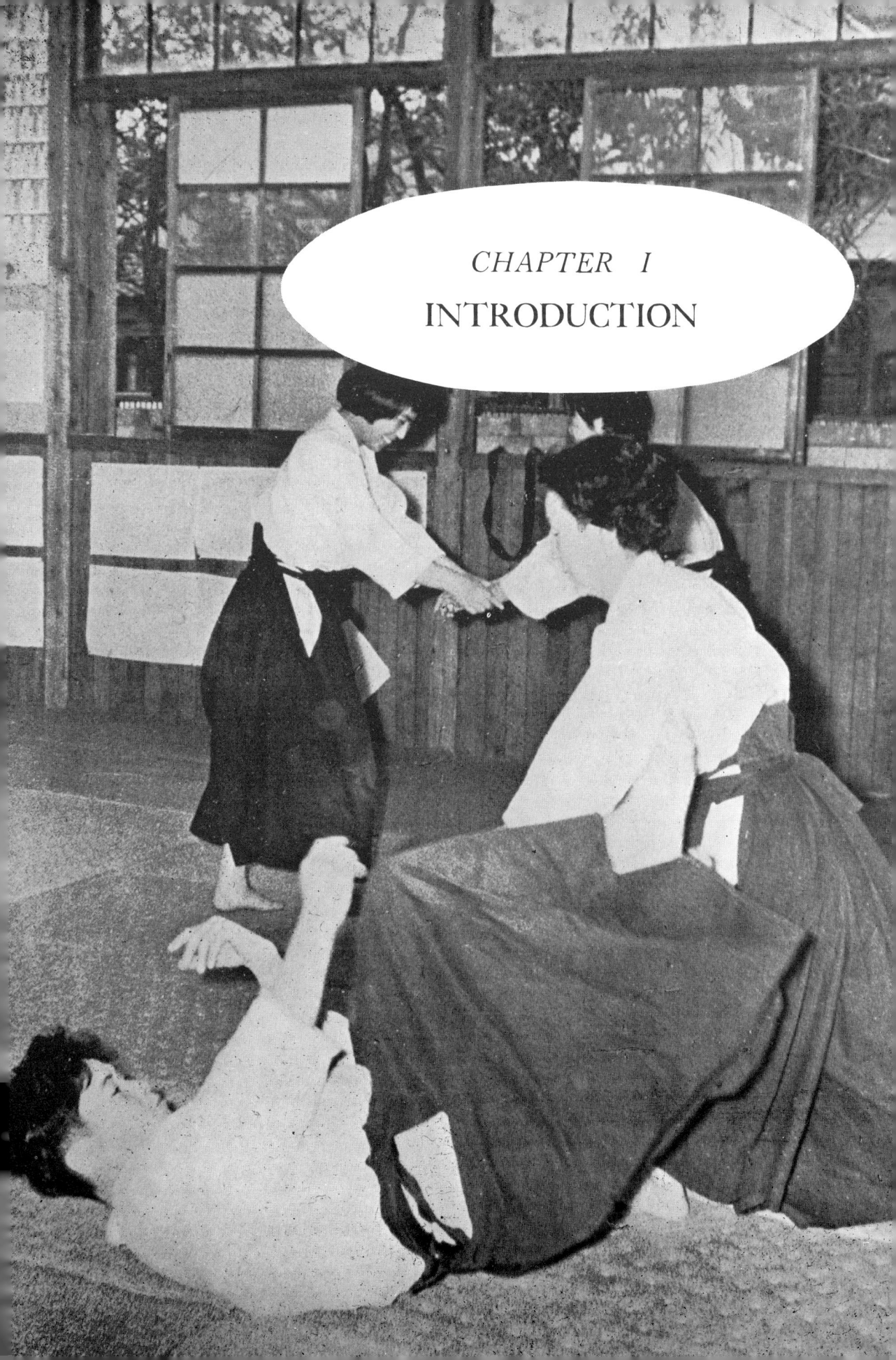

AIKIDO reveals to us the path to one-ness with Heaven and Earth.

Since ancient times, *Jujutsu*, *Kenjutsu* and *Sumo* have been practiced in Japan to such an extent that even little children have some knowledge about these arts. Together they were called the ancient martial arts.

As conditions changed, *Jujutsu* and *Kenjutsu* became altered to suit the times into *Judo* and *Kendo*. Then from China came *Kempo* and from Okinawa *Karate*. Each of these arts has its devotees and all are assidously practiced. Fifty years ago, the principles of *AIKIDO* were originated by its founder, Professor Morihei Uyeshiba. Its secrets have not been made generally known and even today in Japan only a comparatively few know them. Lately *AIKIDO* has become a topic of general conversation and the name of *AIKIDO*, through newspapers, radio, television, magazines and other media, has become quite familiar, but even among those who have personally seen or practiced it, the number of those who know its true significance is small.

A stream that does not have a clear source cannot have a clear outlet. He who would understand *AIKIDO* correctly, practice it correctly and gain a correct knowledge of it, must pursue its fundamental truths and then build upon this base of truth. It should be emphasized at the beginning that to learn merely the art of *AIKIDO* does not mean that one can attain the exquisite skill that complete mastery brings.

AIKIDO AND NATURE

Mankind affirms the omnipotence of Nature. From such large bodies as the sun, moon and stars to such small objects as a tree, a blade of grass or a piece of wood, all are manifestations of Nature's power. We may call it God or Buddha or Eternal Truth but men everywhere revere Nature's almighty power.

To learn Nature's secret of power, we may turn to philosophy or to religion in an effort to gain similar power for ourselves.

Science recognizes that Mother Nature jealously guards many secrets yet undiscovered and through research hopes to learn more and more. It is not strange that great scientists are often devout believers in a divine power.

Nature's power is so great, so strong yet so close to us. Her truths are revealed to us in even the smallest event, such as the falling of a leaf from a shrub. Not even for a moment could we exist without the operation of her laws. If the law of gravity ceased to work, our bodies would float weightlessly and we would die.

As a fish in water is not conscious of the element in which it lives, we receive the bounties of Nature and take things so much for granted that we become oblivious of her.

All truths are discovered by those whose eyes are opened to observe Mother Nature. All the cardinal points that govern our lives must emanate from our heart's thankfulness to her for her great gifts to us.

The martial arts begin with gratitude and end with gratitude. If there is an error at the important starting point, the martial arts can become dangerous to others and merely brutal fighting arts. Civilization then becomes a murderous weapon with which one nation threatens another.

AIKIDO strives truly to understand Nature, to be grateful for her wonderful gifts to us, to make her heart its heart, and to become one with her. This striving for understanding and the practical application of the laws of Nature, expressed in the words *Ai* and *Ki*, form the fundamental concept of the art of *AIKIDO*.

Indeed, it was the starting point of the founder himself, and it is the reason that although he is nearly 80 years old, he continues his studies to perfect the art he originated.

THE SPIRIT OF LOVING PROTECTION FOR ALL NATURE

The Bible says, "God is love."—1 John 4:8. The Buddha too preached mercy toward all living creatures. Yes, Nature is love: all creation expresses the spirit of loving protection. Not only toward human beings but loving protection for all things down to each blade of grass, each shrub. It may be a nameless plant in an unfrequented locality but in its season it blossoms out and Nature's love is poured upon that plant. In the cosmic scheme, all things receive Nature's blessing in equal measure. In return, all things must be equally grateful for these blessings.

Some one may argue that this is a cruel world; why do you call it a loving Nature when she can inflict so much pain?

That pain exists in the world is agreed, but even this is a manifestation of love. For without experiencing pain, we cannot appreciate comfort. Only as we suffer pain and discomfort can we understand ease and comfort. No matter how luxurious the comfort, if we lose our capacity to enjoy it, it no longer comforts us. No matter how delicious the food we eat, if we lose our sense of taste, the finest feast is wasted on us.

If we break Nature's laws, we cannot attain success in any worthy endeavor. We shall some day pay the penalty for our sins. It is of prime importance then for each individual to discipline himself so that he receives Nature's blessings with gratitude and perceives the relative value of each blessing as it is received.

Professor Uyeshiba always says, "The martial arts are based on love." Those who heard this seemingly paradoxical statement received it with suspicion. One student asked, "How can you call it love when you are learning to throw a man, or hit him or give him pain?"

This student was looking at the form and not the spirit of *AIKIDO* whose principles are nothing less than the principles of Nature. In practicing the martial arts, this spirit must always be held paramount in every act.

You are not throwing your opponent for mere personal satisfaction, nor are you throwing him merely for the sake of throwing him, or doing it by brute force. You are throwing him or being thrown by him all in accordance with Nature's laws and you are both improving and helping each other.

It is because you are following Nature's laws that you are able to throw your opponent. If you do not follow them, you will probably fail in your attempt to move him. The antagonists are not wary enemies fighting one another; each is a mirror in which he can see which one is right and which one is wrong. Together they serve as a whetstone for mutual self-improvement. He who seeks to improve only himself, caring naught for anyone else, will never become adept in *AIKIDO*. But he who seeks to improve his opponent polishes his own art and both owe each other thanks for that.

Whether throwing or being thrown, if there is some sense of displeasure in the act, it is time to observe if there has not been some unnatural strain somewhere, some violation of Nature's laws. It will be time also to begin again from the beginning. To throw another without feeling that you are throwing him, to be thrown without feeling that you are being thrown, working as one with your opponent, showing your obedience to Nature's laws in every movement of your bodies, body and spirit invigorated by a magnanimous feeling one for the other, every act in the contest a manifestation of natual love—that is *AIKIDO*.

Those who watch the actual training methods are amazed that *AIKIDO*, unlike the traditional martial arts which seek to overawe the new converts with their prestige strives to practise in earnest but joyfully and harmoniously in unreserved friendliness.

All this serves to prove that *AIKIDO* is one of the martial arts which obey the laws of Nature, and that the spirit and special characteristics spoken of by Professor Uyeshiba, its founder, when he said, "The martial arts are based on love" are given their finest proof by *AIKIDO*.

THE RATIONALE OF NON-RESISTANCE

Today's high degree of civilization is not an unmixed blessing because on the one hand it has contributed largely to man's happiness, and on the other hand as is recognized by all has led man to the folly of conflict. Once war begins, all mankind will be exposed to the danger of annihilation.

We search for Nature's truths; we discover them and by using the basic principles realize the steady advancement of civilization. Yet perversely we abuse the blessings of Nature and plot our own destruction. It is largely because we allowed Nature's truths to guide us that we were able to make inventions and discoveries for our own betterment. Why then use them to destroy ourselves? The answer is, man's incorrigible leaning toward conflict. In all Nature, there is no conflict. Only in man's competitive world is there conflict. If we sincerely seek the secrets of Nature and strive to understand her, we must understand not only the little bits and pieces of truth but the fundamental principles of truth, and put the lessons we learn to practical use.

The spirit of universal love and non-resistance cannot bring on conflict. It is a man who fights for the sake of fighting; man fights to win. Then conflict breeds more conflict. More and more man alienates himself from Nature. He plants the seeds of his own destruction.

There is no one who does not desire peace. But too often this is a desire for a personal peace, limited to one's own immediate surroundings, a greedy, selfish desire, the desire of one who prays to win at all costs, of one who is constantly preparing for conflict.

He who seeks true peace must first understand and endeavor to cultivate the spirit of non-resistance. Simple suppression of one's fighting instinct merely postpones the day when it will burst violently forth. As for one who habitually practices fighting, we know that he cannot control his spirit. To ask one like him to refrain from fighting is just a futile gesture. Only by practicing non-resistance can we inculcate within us the spirit of peace.

It is not easy to avoid conflict in a world such as ours where the survival of the fitter is the rule and the strong preys upon the weak. All around us are conflicts large and small, internal and external. Too many men spend too much of their time planning ways to surpass or overcome others. The polite and the diffident ones must eat their competitor's dust. Those who surrender meekly without fighting are trampled on. The martial arts and most sports make victory the principal end and their practitioners train themselves to win at all cost. Considering all these factors, is it possible for one not to fight while all around him others are fighting?

AIKIDO has the answer to this problem. *AIKIDO* is based on the laws of Nature and believes that "The martial arts express love." That is why so much is made of the principles of non-resistance. Theory and practice thus go hand in hand in *AIKIDO*.

In *AIKIDO*, right is might. You are required only to perform your own mission in life—it is not necessary to think about surpassing or overcoming others. Nor is it necessary to prove that you are strong, because of greater importance is the question of whether you are right or wrong, whether or not you are following the laws.

All the *AIKIDO* arts are involved with the principles of non-resistance. A competitive spirit in you arouses a like spirit in your opponent. No matter how strong he may be, you do not oppose his strength with yours but lead him in the direction of his own strength and throw him. This is *AIKIDO*, explained in great detail in the chapter on *AIKIDO* Techniques and Arts. As you practice them, you will discover for yourself how great a difference there can be in their application when your mind is governed by the spirit of non-resistance and when it is not.

The combative spirit is almost always accompanied by an uneasy state of mind. If a competitor equal in strength with you approaches and merely stands near you, your mind quakes with apprehension. If through your *AIKIDO* experience you understand the principles of non-resistance and have kept up your practice, your mind will be at peace.

CHAPTER II
AIKIDO AND MENTAL AND PHYSICAL COORDINATION

As nature loves and protects all creation and helps all things grow and develop, AIKIDO leads every devotee along the straight and narrow path and strives to teach mankind its truths with all sincerity.

COORDINATION OF MIND AND BODY

AIKIDO is a way of mental and physical coordination. Every movement in *AIKIDO* requires coordination of mind and body, and constant practice is required to maintain absolute stability at all times.

Your mind and body are Nature's gift to you, an inseparable unit that helps you do a true man's job only when fully coordinated. Your mind cannot exist without a body. A body without a mind is no longer a man. Even a baby has a mind.

The body has form and can feel through the five senses, while the mind is formless and cannot feel. The existence of the mind can be seen only through the physical body.

Most persons think of the body first and are apt to forget the important functions of the mind but there are others who think of the importance of the mind and think little of the body. Of course, both viewpoints are wrong. Both mind and body are important, neither being more important than the other, neither being able to operate alone. The palm of one hand cannot make a sound but when two palms are brought together, there is the sound of a clap. It is only when both mind and body are working smoothly together that they can manifest their function. We can all understand co-ordination but do we make practical use of it? We regretfully answer, "No." Many of us use mind and body separately or at cross purposes, cancelling out each other.

Among the rare instances of mental and physical coordination you may have experienced or heard about would be when a fire or other emergency made it necessary to carry objects out of a house. You may have carried out a very heavy object that you could not even lift under ordinary circumstances. In this case, the lifting power did not come from outside. The potential power within you was called forth. Strength was created in a split second by high coordination of mind and body. After the fire, the mind could not be concentrated on the task and physical strength alone could not lift up a heavy object. If coordination is possible, we can create such strength at will and use it in our daily lives.

But to read books while thinking of unrelated subjects, to work unwillingly, to try to sleep with an angry mind, to try to get well while worrying about death, to walk forward while looking backward, to try to convince others while you are becoming angry—these are a few examples of mind and body used separately.

You will find by learning to coordinate mind and body that you have tremendous power not hitherto known to you, that the realization that you can call forth this power at will can calm your mind, and that you enjoy a feeling of gratitude and of being constantly refreshed. You put behind you thoughts of aggressiveness or competition, yet you have the courage to meet dauntlessly all obstacles placed before you.

In *AIKIDO*, every movement becomes art itself, but this is possible only when mind and body are coordinated. One who observes only the bodily movements of *AIKIDO* and ignores the laws of the mind can talk about *AIKIDO* but he actually knows only the shadow of *AIKIDO*. He lacks knowledge in depth.

Since Mother Nature has given us both a mind and a body, it would seem most natural to use them together but we know that this is very difficult to do.

If you were resting without a worry in the world in Nature's broad bosom, your mind and body would easily be coordinated, just as a rough sea, left alone, would soon revert to its original calm.

As you go outdoors on a warm spring day and look at the beauties of Nature all about you, you become absorbed in what you see. Or as you sit under a clear sky at night and watch the stars, you lose your sense of self and of the earth as though you were completely at one with Nature.

It is at such times that your mind and body become one. If we could all continue to have at all times the magnanimity and purity of heart that at-one-ment with Nature would engender in us as we meet people and live our lives, how pleasant this world would be! Unfortunately, such a state of affairs would not last long. Any slight change or vibration would disturb the fine equilibrium and bring us back again into this world of hatred, agony and strife.

The mind may be likened to the surface of water. A mirror-calm pond reflects the true, round moon. A puff of wind ruffles the surface into ripples and the moon is shattered into a thousand golden pieces. The mind is like this. A peaceable, clear, stable mind can make correct judgments, but a disturbed, shaky mind will fail to reflect the true form and color of what it sees. It cannot see that willow leaves are green or that roses are red. If you would see Nature in all her truth and understand that truth, you must first coordinate your mind and body and reach such a state that your entire body is like a polished mirror. It is impossible to grasp the truths of Nature if your mind and body are at odds with each other.

Many sages since ancient times have pointed out the need of mental and physical coordination and told us that to keep the formless, intangible human mind in tune with the physical body is one of the difficult things in life.

Even as we sit quiet and relaxed, we do not find it easy to keep the mind at rest. It is even more difficult to keep the mind calm while the body is in motion or exercising. From ages past, men seeking the truths of Nature first tried to train their minds to think clearly by going into solitude. They sat on rocks, or remained under a waterfall as they disciplined their minds. Some accomplished their purpose; others lost their lives in vain. In our day, it is almost impossible to undertake such training unless one is independently wealthy and has much leisure.

How then can the average man train himself in coordination? One way is near at hand. It required many years of unremitting exploration and training to discover this way.

Now that it has been revealed, let us see whether or not it is a way that can be reached by daily training. If it is not, it is not a true way.

AIKIDO is no exception to this rule. Founder Professor Uyeshiba discovered and opened the way to mental and physical training as part of the daily life of any one in our modern world who has the will and determination. How then in *AIKIDO* can such a difficult task as mental and physical coordination be accomplished?

RELATION BETWEEN MIND AND BODY

AIKIDO is a way to train, study and understand through practice in our daily lives a method of mental and physical coordination. There are those who think of *AIKIDO* as an art to throw an attacking opponent in a split second, or to hold down a strong man with only one finger. They think of *AIKIDO* as a highly developed self-defense art. This is a superficial view. *AIKIDO* is not merely an art to throw others but a way to apply the laws of Nature to our daily lives. One who does not understand this does not truly understand *AIKIDO*.

How can mental and physical coordination in *AIKIDO* be made a part of our lives?

Before we answer this question, one thing must be clearly understood. It is difficult to try to coordinate mind and body unless there is a definite objective in mind. Mind and body each has its own laws and in order to make them coordinate, one must subordinate itself to the other. It cannot be a half-hearted yielding of leadership. The question then is, which should be the master, mind or body? Shall mind control body? Or body control mind? The method of training and the way of thinking will differ according to the decision that is reached. You have heard the phrase, "A sound mind in a sound body."

There are many people who have taken this seriously and built up a strong body and possess a sound mind. There are others who believe this: they are physically strong but mentally weak, and still others who can throw their opponents but cannot control their own mind.

If the body is master and can control the mind, life become very simple, and the existing sports and martial arts may be relied on to teach coordination of mind and body. In reality, it is not so easy.

Though your body may be healthy and strong, it becomes weak with age or when you suffer from illness. The body is a living entity and is influenced by its surroundings. The mind, controlled by a body which is constantly swayed by external influences, would then be uneasy and unstable. Where everything runs smoothly and the body is full of vigor, you are strong and vigorous. But you seem unable to accomplish anything when you are frustrated and low in spirit. It is necessary to possess a truly strong mind that can rise above unfavorable circumstances and meet fearlessly every possible obstacle. This requires training of not only the body but also the mind. Naturally it cannot be said that the body is master.

AIKIDO believes that mind is master. Every follower of *AIKIDO* must study the laws of mind, train his mind, letting the body follow and find a way to coordinate itself with the mind. *AIKIDO* recognizes that the condition of the body affects the mind. When the body is in poor condition, the spirit is low. *AIKIDO* believes that when the body suffers from illness, the mind necessarily suffers too. When the body is unhappy, the mind is likewise unhappy. *AIKIDO* strives to strengthen the mind by training so that it cannot be influenced by surroundings that affect the body. No matter how much you train, there is a limit to what the physical body can be taught to do. The mind, on the other hand, has no form or color and has an unlimited capacity for learning if you train it. You can make your mind stronger as age advances. Those who devote themselves to developing only their bodies and the arts will find it difficult when they reach old age to compete with young men and win. The founder of *AIKIDO*, Professor Uyeshiba, is now 80 years old and still continues *AIKIDO* instruction. In a fraction of a minute, he throws several strong men who attack him simultaneously with staves. If you were to see him moving about freely as though performing a Japanese dance, throwing young men at will, you would wonder if he is actually such an old man, and be lost in admiration. Of all the many students he has trained, none can throw him or even touch him.

See Professor Uyeshiba's performance and realize the importance of training the mind. He has a powerful yet serene mind and he advances in his art as he grows older.

TRAINING OF MIND AND BODY

In the preceding section, I have explained that mental and physical coordination can be accomplished by making mind the master and letting the body follow. I shall explain how that functioning of the mind affects the body. Merely to say in the abstract sense that mind is the master avails nothing if this cannot be put into practice. I shall, therefore, show a few examples as a guide for daily training.

Example 1

One man stands as in Photos 1 and 2.

In Photo 1, he puts strength into his entire body and lets another push him gently

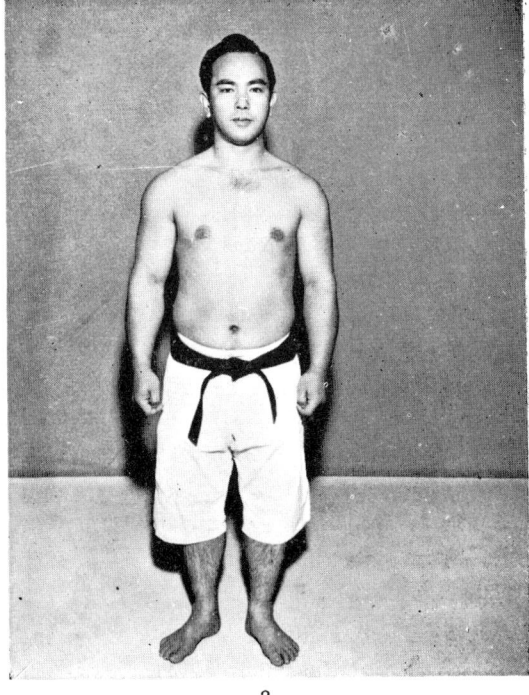

3   4

either from the front or the back. The standing man, of course, tries not to be pushed off balance.

Next standing as in Photo 2, he lets the other push him.

Compare closely the difference in the pushing power that must be exerted in 1 and 2.

In Photo 2, the man concentrates his mind on the one point, a point about two inches below the navel, which I shall explain in the next section. He does not put physical strength into the one point. If he did, the result would be the same as in Photo 1. He keeps his shoulder completely relaxed and lets his arms fall naturally. If somebody pushes him by the shoulder, he continues to concentrate his mind on the one point. He thinks neither about being pushed nor about the one who pushes him. He concentrates only on the one point.

Any one who tries this experiment will readily understand. In the case of Photo 1, the person standing appears very strong and he himself may feel strong, but in reality, he can be moved by even a slight push. On the other hand, in Photo 2, you see one who appears not to be exerting strength and he himself feels weak, yet he stands firmly as if reinforced by steel.

Photo 1 shows an effect of physical strength, and Photo 2 shows stability of mind. To keep the mind stable requires concentration of mind on the center of the lower abdomen, and I shall explain this matter in the next section.

Example 2

As the Photo illustrates, A stands erect and B places both hands under A's armpits and lifts him up.

Just as in Example 1, let us try this two ways.

First, A puts strength into his muscles and in addition thinks about the top of his head.

Let us say that A weighs 150 pounds and that B can lift over 200 pounds. Naturally, B can lift A easily. B judges A's weight to be about 150 pounds, but B feels that A's weight is much less because A is thinking about the top of his head.

Next A concentrates his mind on the one point, or his lower abdomen, keeps his mind stable even when some one tries to lift him, and stands calm and natural. This time when B tries to lift A, he feels a much heavier weight. To keep the mind stable is difficult, but after the one in A's place goes through training, B though he has great strength may feel that A's weight is too great for him to lift.

We know that it is impossible to change the body weight at will. Example 2 shows the effect which the mind can have on the body. When a training partner tries to lift you, your mind goes up. Though you put on strength, you cannot change your body weight and your effort will not affect your partner at all. If you concentrate your mind on the one point and keep your mind calm and stable, your body becomes hard to lift up. Practice makes perfect. Learn through actual experience.

Example 3

Photo 5: A makes a fist, bends his arm at the elbow and puts strength into the arm.

Photo 7: B puts one hand to A's elbow and the other hand to A's fist and tries to bend the arm back toward the shoulder, A increases the strength he is putting into his arm to prevent B from bending it.

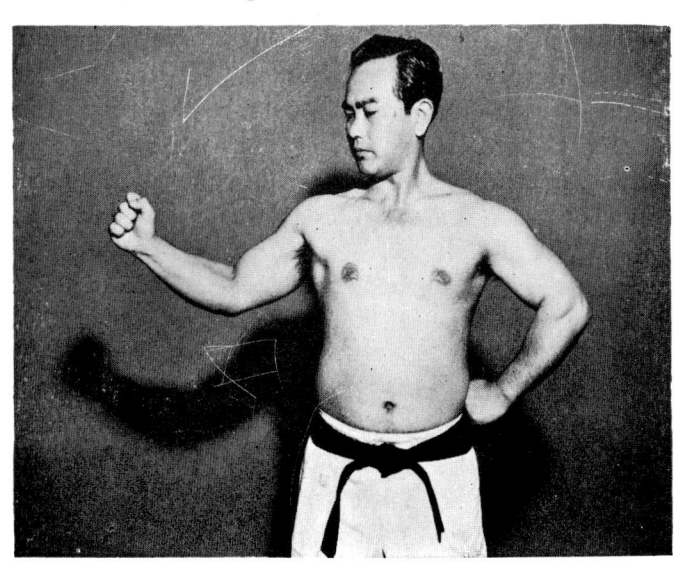

Photo 6: A puts his arm in the same angle as in Photo 5, opens his fingers and does not put any strength into his arm. Photo 8: As B tries to bend the arm, A does not let his mind think about B's strength. He thinks only of his own strength passing through the lower part of his arm, spurting out and reaching to the ends of the earth, and

continues to think that at all times.

In Photo 5, if A and B are of equal strength, the arm will surely bend. Because the elbow joint is already slightly bent to begin with and is made to bend.

In Photo 8, though A keeps the arm at the same angle, B will discover that the arm is unbendable as though it were an iron bar. If B tries harder, A can smile with confidence as he watches B since he does not need to put any greater strength into his arm.

This shows the effect of mind over body. Photo 5, shows reliance on the strength of a man's arm: Photo 6 shows reliance on physical strength plus mental power.

You now understand that physical strength plus mental power creates extraordinary strength. The human mind though formless is truly a source of power. When water gushes out of a fire hose, that hose cannot be bent. When water is shut off, the hose can be bent easily, rolled up and carried away.

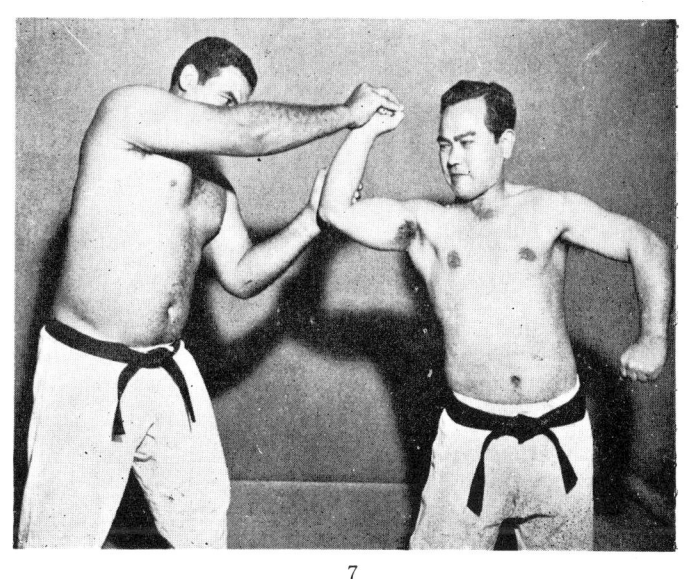

In Example 3, the arm is a fire hose and the mind is the water. Concentrated thinking creates actual power, makes the arm strong and unbendable. If thinking stops, the arm has only its ordinary strength.

In *AIKIDO*, we call it an Unbendable Arm, and the poses shown in Examples 1 and 2 are known as Immovable Postures.

These poses, apparently without strength, are yet powerful postures. If you keep your body tense, you cannot move swiftly in an emergency. If you are relaxed, you can move fast, but there is no strength with this speed. In *AIKIDO*, you practice keeping a strong posture without apparent strength and being prepared to meet any change in case of emergency. There is a constant endeavor to maintain the Immovable Posture and the Unbendable Arm, fundamental postures which enable you to use mind and body in coordination.

It is impossible to put strength into the entire body and practice for even one hour. In *AIKIDO*, your body is relaxed without strength and you can practice all day without tiring, and you will enjoy practice or work and your efficiency will increase.

Through such easy daily training, you attain a fundamental understanding of all the *AIKIDO* arts, which will be discussed in later chapters, and you will be taking your first step in mental and physical coordination.

It is so easy that old men, women and children can practice.

AIKIDO training and discipline, however, are not so easy as they look. To keep your mind in the lower part of your abdomen and keep the other parts of your body relaxed is easy for any one to do, so simple that one is apt to neglect training.

The mind is formless and free to move. Merely continuing to think of the one point makes the mind stay there. This is not hard to do.

One thing must be remembered: the mind can easily move to the one point and at the same time can quickly and easily wander from there. To repeat, mental and physical coordination is easy but disturbance of this coordination is also easy. Therefore, pay much attention to daily practice until mental and physical coordination become a habit.

It is easy to understand the theory, but it is difficult to put it into practice. If you really want to understand coordination of mind and body, it will be well first to determine to keep up your effort and practice daily as you enjoy it.

SEIKA-NO-ITTEN   (*The One Point*)

Let me explain about the one point in the center of the lower abdomen.

From ancient times in the Orient, this one point has been called *Seika-No-Itten*, and is regarded as of primary importance. Buddhism, especially of the Zen sect, which is lately being studied and practiced in the United States of America, is devoted entirely to training in *Seika Tanden*. India's Yoga may be said to be based on this Seika Tanden training.

Seika Tanden is the basis of mental and physical coordination. To attain the principles of Nature, mind and body must be coordinated and in order to coordinate mind and body this *Seika-No-Itten* or the one point must be understood. In *AIKIDO*, it is absolutely necessary to understand the one point, or real *AIKIDO* arts cannot be understood.

Why then this emphasis on the one point?

Sounds have sound waves, and light has light waves. No one will deny that sound and light waves have power. The mind that controls man is actual power that exists. The mind has mind waves.

The constant functioning of the cerebrum and cerebellum in man generates these mind waves. It is not strange to learn then that the energy of these mind waves creates great power.

If you would have your mind function with greater efficiency, you must concentrate your mind waves, not dissipate them as when you are trying to think about something to your right as well as to your left, or studying while you are thinking about playing. If you do this, the mind waves will be unable to create any kind of strength.

The mind must be concentrated instantaneously on problems directly as they arise, and yet must not cling to them. A mirror reflects an image instantly, but if the object that it is reflecting is taken away, no image remains. If the previous image were to remain, the mirror could not reflect a second object clearly. Concentrate your mind instantaneously on a problem but do not cling to it—and you have real concentration. To concentrate the mind on one object and cling to it may look like concentration. It is not—it is attachment.

Concentration can cause attachment. If you try to avoid attachment, concentration becomes impossible. When you are surrounded by many men and you watch the movement of the one just in front of you, you cannot see the other opponents' movements. If you pay attention to every one, you will leave an opening for one of them. You must be able to keep your mind calm, to concentrate your mind for the briefest instant to front or back, left or right, to every direction and to detect the slightest move of an opponent. This concentration of attention must leap from one to another of the opponents who make significant moves. Because you concentrate instantly on individuals, you constantly change your position. You in effect deal with one opponent at a time. To concentrate your attention on one man and attach your mind on him would be fatal.

Such a scene as the foregoing is easy to talk about but difficult to put into practice. Hard training is required to attain such a state of proficiency.

We might say that the mind gives shelter to the body. In order to keep the mind to one spot, it must be concentrated somewhere. That place is *Seika-No-Itten*. Every object falls if released. The center of gravity is always low. You know that even without hearing an explanation of Newton's law of gravity. If you relax your body, your strength naturally settles lower in your body. To concentrate on the head or on the shoulder is contrary to the laws of Nature. If you concentrate your mind on the lower part of the upper body, the strength in your shoulders goes down and power will rest where it should.

Seika-No-Itten is a point of intersection of mind and body. It is where the laws of mind and body are joined together. Mental and physical coordination is possible only when a calm mind is centered on *Seika-No-Itten*. Concentration on the head and stiff shoulders will prevent mental and physical coordination.

Here another problem arises. If the mind is concentrated at all times on *Seika-No-Itten*, it is impossible in this busy world to think of anything else. True. You cannot even converse with others. The mind should be concentrated on all things instantaneously and should not be attached to any one thing.

How can this be done?

If you concentrate your mind on *Seika-No-Itten*, relax your shoulders, complying with all the other points mentioned in Example 1, your posture will be strong and you will feel at ease. It is under such conditions that you must perform all your daily acts. You will then be in a state of mental and physical coordination, and your endeavor will be to continue to feel that you are in such a state. It would be well if in the end, without conscious thought, you are able to perform your daily acts in such a state.

At first, this state of being is easily disturbed. If you become aware that you are not in this state, you can think of the one point and create this condition again. You can gradually lengthen the time you are in this state and finally you will be able to continue this state of being even in your sleep.

When you reach this stage of development, everything can be done by the power of mental and physical coordination and you can use your new power to your heart's content. When you are confronted by problems, you can at any time demonstrate your ability, often to your own amazement.

Such training, if there is a will, can be done as part of your daily life. Even a small effort each day when it is accumulated adds up to respectable power. This may be slow but it is sure; continue to train diligently.

The attainment of higher stages of development in *AIKIDO* makes it possible to make innumerable variations of movement. If this state is disturbed, you cannot throw your opponent but you can both at once analyze your own mistakes. If you apply art under such a condition, you can throw your opponent or be thrown by him with a pleasant feeling. If the condition is disturbed, you feel that something is wrong somewhere. If you find wherein the mistake lies, you and your training partner can correct this and both of you advance together in the art.

It is easy enough to maintain such a condition when you remain quiet, but it is much more difficult when innumerable variations of movement are required. To make such a difficult thing easier is one of the superior characteristics of the *AIKIDO* arts.

So much for *AIKIDO* principles, based on the laws of Nature. Before going into the methods of actual *AIKIDO* training, I shall write briefly about the originator of *AIKIDO*, Professor Morihei Uyeshiba.

CHAPTER III
PROFESSOR MORIHEI UYESHIBA

There is no discord in the absolute truth of nature, but there is discord in the realm of relative truth. AIKIDO is in accord with Nature.

Let us suppose that there is a steep mountain as yet unconquered. Though many have tried to reach its summit, only a few have even reached half way. Some lost their way; some lost their lives, but many fortunately returned without mishap. Then came a man of iron will, intrepidity, determination and cool contemplation. With inflexible spirit and knowledge of the mountain based on the experience of his predecessors, he finally attained the summit through his supreme effort.

He spent a lifetime to reach this summit. Then he looked back and opened a way to others by the sign posts he left behind. Today, anybody may climb this mountain without losing his way and may enjoy the same thrill he enjoyed.

If a trail-blazer had not shown the way to the summit, one who came later not only would be unable to climb the mountain but would be unable to judge whether or not the way he was walking was right or wrong. Who would not express his gratitude for what this trail-blazer had done?

We feel the same gratitude to one who blazes a trial for our lives. Many people worship Jesus Christ and others believe in Buddha, because they enjoy the benevolent influence of these great teachers.

It is the same in *AIKIDO*. Those who through *AIKIDO* wish to understand the laws of Nature and put them into practice must first express their gratitude for what Professor Uyeshiba has done and must engrave his name in their hearts. Therefore, I shall present a brief sketch of Professor Uyeshiba's life.

He was born in Wakayama prefecture in Japan. In his childhood, he was sickly and weak, and nobody could have imagined his becoming a man of robust health and the founder of such a superior art which startled all Japan. He made up his mind to train his body through the martial arts. The orignator of *AIKIDO*, in which spiritual discipline and mental training are highly regarded, at first like all the rest trained himself only on the physical level.

He practiced almost all the existing martial arts, beginning with *Kito-ryu Jujutsu, Yagyu-ryu, Aioi-ryu Hozoin-ryu* and finally *Daito-ryu*. Whatever he thought was best, even modern gymnastics, *Judo, Kendo*, bayonet arts, he took up and studied at every opportunity. He wandered from place to place seeking teachers, and spent his inheritance in this way.

During his training period, he showed the utmost courtesy to his teachers, even preparing food for them. Once training started, he devoted himself completely to his task. In his adolescence, he was only five feet one inch tall yet weighed 165 pounds. His formerly weak body became as strong as iron. His undeviating determination was to devote himself to training so that he could triumph over all others.

During the Russo-Japanese War (1904–1905), he volunteered for service in the Japanese army, fighting at the front and testing his own strength and his command over the arts. He then went to Hokkaido and worked as a foreman of the immigrants. Even while engaged in farming, his obsession was his training in the martial arts.

With only a *bokken* (wooden sword), he wandered all over Japan and if he found one superior to him, remained with him as a pupil and trained until he had learned all that he could learn from him, then moved on. He became the most proficient man in the martial arts in Japan. In fact, he was invincible.

However, just as he was about to accomplish his goal, some doubt grew in his mind, not on the individual arts themselves but rather on all martial arts in general. To throw others, to strike them down, to fight and prevail over them—of what use is it all, anyway? he asked. If this is all that the martial arts mean to us, of what value are they?

To win means that some day we shall lose. Today's victor will be the vanquished tomorrow.

You are physically strong in your youth, but your strength wanes with advancing age and a younger man will overcome you. Today you are in the prime of life and can enjoy the feeling that comes in overcoming others, but the time will surely come when you yourself will be overcome. Because others lose, you win. Such victories are relative. Is there such a thing as absolute victory?

Even though you are victorious, what does this do for you? In the eyes of Nature, to win or lose in the world of men looks valueless, of no more meaning than the ebb and flow of the waves on the shore. Was it not a waste of energy to put a lifetime of effort into such a thing?

You may subdue others; you may not be able to control your own mind. If you cannot control your mind at will, winning over others will not bring you happiness. Your vanity may be satisfied, but what benefit does this bring to mankind in general?

Once the doubt grew, it led to others and finally to endless doubts about everything. Professor Uyeshiba, once he starts anything, puts his whole soul into it until it is completed. This time he laid the martial arts aside and put his entire energy to resolving his doubts.

He knocked at the doors of famous temples and he studied philosophy. He went into solitude and meditated. He remained under a waterfall to open "The eyes of his soul." Determined to solve his problem, he continued his ascetic life. Alone on a mountain, swinging his wooden sword, he became absorbed in the question, "What is martial art?"

After some years of training and pilgrimages, he came down one day from a mountain, entered the yard of a cottage, poured water over his body and looked up into the blue sky. Suddenly at this moment he felt strangely inspired. He was uplifted, simply delighted as tears rolled down his cheeks in an expression of gratitude to heaven and earth. In a flash of light, he perceived the truth. He realized that he had became one with the Universe.

"Seek, and ye shall find." He sought the truth earnestly, and endeavored painstakingly to find the answer to his question, and God willed that he should find it. At last, with mind and body, he experienced the great truth of Nature. Now he surrendered his small ego and made the spirit of Nature his own mind.

This may be called a revelation of God, a state of perception of the absolute truth, as Zen calls it.

Professor Uyeshiba, recalling the events of that day, always tells the story as follows:

"As I was strolling in the yard, the earth suddenly trembled. Golden vapor gushed out of the earth enveloping my body, and then I felt myself turning into a golden body. At the same time, my mind and body felt light; I could understand what the chirping birds were saying and I understood clearly the creator's spirit.

"It was precisely at that moment that I received enlightenment: the fundamental principle of the martial arts is God's love and universal love. Tears of ecstacy rolled down my cheeks. From that time on, I have felt that the entire earth is my home and the sun and stars are mine. Neither position, nor fame, nor honors, nor wealth, nor the desire to become more powerful than others have any attraction for me—these have all vanished away.

"The martial arts are not concerned with brute force to knock opponents down, nor with lethal weapons that lead the world into destruction. The true martial arts, without struggling, regulate the *Ki* of the universe, guard the peace of the world, and produce and bring to maturity everything in nature.

"Therefore, martial training is not training that has as its primary purpose the defeating of others, but practice of God's love within ourselves."

Since then, Professor Uyeshiba has taken great pains to express this lofty feeling. He learned that it is impossible to reveal such a feeling of mind and body through the martial arts and other methods that existed at that time. Since he was trying to express the spirit of heaven and earth, there would have to be a new kind of arts which would be capable of manifesting the will of Nature.

Thus the martial arts practiced by Professor Uyeshiba changed from day to day and finally evolved into this new creation which is the *AIKIDO* of today.

The violent and fierce arts previously practiced, which crushed everything changed into gentle, harmonious arts, which tenderly embraced all things. Professor Uyeshiba moves with grace as though he were performing a Japanese dance, seemingly oblivious of the existence of his opponent. He throws in a second several strong men and yet those who are thrown do not know how it was done. His every movement is in accord with the laws of Nature, and the power of the opponent who leaps at him goes back inevitably to the opponent himself. He has thus attained a state of absolute non-resistance.

"Nature is broad and profound. The more you advance, the more you see ahead of you. *AIKIDO* is a way without end, harmonious with Nature."

"I am just in the first grade in *AIKIDO* and I am still practicing it. I will continue to do so all the rest of my life and leave *AIKIDO* as an inheritance for the generations to come."

Thus Professor Uyeshiba expresses his belief humbly and quietly and puts his belief into practice as he preaches.

Admirals such as Isamu Takeshita, Sankichi Takahashi, Hidesuke Yamamoto, and other flag officers received instruction from him. Men of noble families such as Sameshima and Matsudaira were also among his students.

These students undoubtedly admired his unrivaled mastery of the arts, but they were even more attracted to his mentality and distinguished personality.

When World War II began, Professor Uyeshiba for reasons of his own left the

Dojo, built a hut in the mountains of Ibaragi prefecture and engaged in farming. After that, for twelve years he devoted himself to mental training.

During this period he did not accept any new pupils, but he brought up a few of the students who were deeply attached to him and went to his mountain hut.

I am one of the fortunate few who are privileged to have close communion with the Professor's personality and receive the mental discipline of *AIKIDO*.

For some time after the War, Professor Uyeshiba remained in the mountains and devoted himself leisurely to his training. He saw that post-war morality was at a low ebb among the people and many young men went astray, and he deeply grieved at this tendency. Many self-conceited Japanese who had thought themselves spiritually superior lost self-confidence after the miserable defeat of their nation and even denied the existence of any spirit.

Professor Uyeshiba was convinced that this was the time to open *AIKIDO* to the public, let them know the proper use of mind and body, let them understand the principles of Nature and let them once more gain back their confidence. He called his former students together and began the spread of *AIKIDO*.

Today in Japan many young men and even old men devote themselves day and night to *AIKIDO* training. *AIKIDO* is also studied in America, France, India and Burma, and many come from all over the world to the headquarters *Dojo* in Tokyo and ask for instruction from Professor Uyeshiba.

The headquarters *Dojo*, located at No. 102, Wakamatsu-cho, Shinjuku-ku, Tokyo, Japan, is currently operated by the Professor's son, Kisshomaru Uyeshiba, of the eighth rank in *AIKIDO*.

Professor Uyeshiba appears sometimes at this *Dojo* and himself instructs the young men.

I received permission from Professor Uyeshiba to spread *AIKIDO* in America. First I went to Hawaii, started *AIKIDO* instruction, and organized Hawaii Aiki Kwai. Over 2000 men practice *AIKIDO* and there are over 100 *Yudansha* (black belt holders), and *AIKIDO* is being spread to the mainland United States.

In France, there is an instructor, who has attained the sixth rank in *AIKIDO*. He has given *AIKIDO* instruction for the past six years and is continuing to train many students. Some of them went especially to Japan, remained at the headquarters *Dojo* for a year practicing *AIKIDO*.

The spirit of universal love and the rationale of non-resistance are being understood by people all over the world today. It can be said that Professor Uyeshiba's long-cherished desire to contribute even a little to world peace has been fulfilled.

He was, incidentally, awarded the *Medal of Honor with Purple Ribbon** in 1960. In the following year, on the invitation of Hawaii Aiki Kwai, he went there on the occasion of the completion of Hawaii Aiki Kwaikan, and performed his expert art besides giving invaluable instructions.

 * An Honor awarded to those who have outstandingly contributed toward furtherance of learning, arts, invention, creative work, etc.

CHAPTER IV
THE ARTS OF AIKIDO

Do not criticize any of the other martial arts. Speak ill of others and it will surely come back to you. The mountain does not laugh at the river because it is lowly, nor does the river speak ill of the mountain because it cannot move about.

ATTITUDE TOWARD TRAINING

1. Continue To Practice Earnestly

No matter what art you are trying to master, continued earnest practice is of primary importance. This is especially so in learning *AIKIDO*, because it concerns itself with mental matters to a greater degree than any other art. Usually a talented man may leave others behind even though he may not put in as many hours in practice, and if he be a powerful man, he will be able to overcome his opponents even though he may not train himself as rigorously as they.

In *AIKIDO* training, however, even a clever man cannot hope to master the various arts to be able to use them when the real occasion arises if he does not continue to practice with a purpose. He may say to himself after hearing an explanation, "So that's what non-resistance means," and feel that he truly understands. He only thinks he understand; usually he forgets very soon all that he has heard.

When the time comes to use the arts of *AIKIDO*, you will move by reflex action if you have practiced correctly. Conscious action is slow, while subconscious action is extremely fast. In *AIKIDO*, you will learn always to coordinate your use of mind and body. For this, it is not enough to understand the arts with the conscious mind only. Practice of the arts must be continued to the point where each art is beaten into the subconscious mind. *Aiki Taiso* (*Aiki* exercises) will be explained later in this book. They were prepared so that those who can practice by themselves will find them of benefit. If the movements shown are repeated often enough the conscious movements will become subconscious movements and will be expressed as reflex actions when the time comes to use them.

Our consciousness is made up of material arising out of our subconscious, which in turn is made up of past experiences, acquired knowledge, memory and so on. Our subconscious always controls our conscious thoughts.

For example, let us think about a glass. We have seen and used glasses before so we know about how much this glass costs, whether it is cheap or expensive, that it will break if dropped, that we use it to drink water or iced tea, and so on—knowledge gained from past experience. Show a glass to a person who has never seen one before. His mind will grasp only the image that his eyes see and nothing more. The picture he gets is still only a visual picture; it is only on the conscious level. Apparently our subconscious is a warehouse of memories.

Using old lumber, we cannot build a fine house. A fine building requires fine building material.

If we would have lofty thoughts, we need first of all to change the material that makes up our mind, our subconscious, and strive to make our thinking lofty. One who is quick-tempered has a subconscious mind full of material that will make him angry. If anything untoward happens, this material leaps to the fore, defeating any effort on the part of the conscious mind to suppress or control it. If one wishes not to become angry, one must change the contents of one's subconscious mind. This can be done if one goes about it intelligently and purposefully.

In *AIKIDO*, it is not enough to say, "Oh, sure! I understand," and be satisfied with a brief encounter with the arts. Continued practice of every movement until it becomes second nature to respond correctly even when attacked suddenly, resulting from a radical change of content of our subconscious mind, is the end toward which the *AIKIDO* practitioner must work. Finally, we can reach a point where we advance as far as our mind wishes us to go without passing beyond the rules set for us by *AIKIDO*.

This is the reason for *AIKIDO's* demanding especially earnest practice.

2. Have a Receptive, Open-Minded Attitude

Truly to learn anything, one must study with a receptive, open-minded attitude. This is especially true in studying *AIKIDO*.

If you pour water into a glass that is already full of tea, most of it will be spilt. If you pour a glassful of water into an empty glass, all of it will go into the glass. If a mind is full of preconceived notions and shallow thoughts, that mind will be incapable of receiving any new thoughts, no matter how lofty the ideas may be.

What you will do in *AIKIDO* is often completely opposed to methods that man has so far employed in the ordinary course of events. It is as though one used to the speed of sound suddenly is confronted with supersonic speed.

In *AIKIDO*, you step from the world of the body to the world of the mind, from the world of aggression to the world of non-resistance. It is quite obvious then that there must be a change in the rules, too.

Empty your mind, therefore, of all preconceived notions that you may have had about *AIKIDO* so that you will be able to receive its principles and accept its truths.

3. Rules During Practice

Rules posted in the *Dojo* at *AIKIDO* headquarters in *Tokyo*:

1) One blow in *AIKIDO* is capable of killing an opponent. In practice, obey your instructor, and do not make practice a time for needless testing of strength.

2) *AIKIDO* is an art in which one man learns to face many opponents simultaneously and requires therefore that you polish and perfect your execution of each movement so that you can take on not only the one directly before you but also those in every direction around you.

3) Practice at all times with a feeling of pleasurable exhilaration.

4) The teachings of your instructor constitute only a small fraction of what you will learn. Your mastery of each movement will depend almost completely on your earnest practice.

5) The daily practice begins with light movements of the body, gradually increasing in intensity and strength, but there must be no overexertion. That is why even an elderly man can continue to practice without bodily harm but with pleasure and profit and will attain the purpose of his training.

6) The purpose of *AIKIDO* is to train both body and mind and to make a man sincere. All *AIKIDO* arts are secret in nature and are not to be revealed publicly nor taught to rogues who will use them for evil purposes.

Of the foregoing rules, that which prohibits revealing the arts to others without good reason was enforced until World War II. After the War, the founder wished to introduce *AIKIDO* to all the world and allowed public demonstration of the arts.

In addition to the six rules, students have been cautioned that the occasion when *AIKIDO* may be used are as follows:

1) When one is in personal danger.
2) When one sees someone else in danger.
3) At a large meeting, when a small number of rogues is making a nuisance of themselves and inconveniencing or endangering the public.

Even in the situation in which the use of *AIKIDO* is sanctioned, such sanctions are not absolute. Every effort must first be made after calm thought to settle matters peaceably. Only when such efforts seem useless should the arts of *AIKIDO* be used.

Any one who has learned the principles of non-resistance and still prefers fighting is considered a failure as a student.

In summary, while you are training yourself, receive your instructor's words earnestly and obediently; learn the basic principles well; practice cheerfully and correctly.

Strive to build within yourself a noble character. Be broadminded. Learn the arts; master them and make them a part of your being. Your efforts are not for personal aggrandizement but that, as one candle can light 10,000 other candles, you may be able to lead people everywhere in the world to a brighter, more cheerful existence.

AIKI TAISO (*AIKI* EXERCISES)

Aiki Taiso is not merely physical exercise that coordinates mind and body. It is not for form alone but can be put to practical use and is called exercise because the movements can be practiced solo, these movements being the same as those used in the various arts of *AIKIDO*. Those used oftenest in the arts during practice have been adapted for *Aiki Taiso*.

While the students are excercising, the instructor will test them from time to time as to their coordination of mind and body and lead them into doing the exercises correctly.

1. Nikyo (Nikajo)

Imagine that your arm is a short length of water hose, your mind, water and your wrist, a nozzle. If you want to spray water at will, you must move the nozzle freely. If you want to extend your mind through your arm in any direction at will, your wrist must be limber yet strong. *Aiki Taiso* Nos. 1, 2 and 3 are for training the wrists. Stand naturally with shoulders relaxed and your mind concentrated on the one point.

At the count of One, twist your left wrist outward and with your right hand help to twist it even more.

At Two, Three, Four and Five, repeat the same motion at each count. Count to Five again, this time twisting the right wrist and helping with the left hand.

At first, you may feel a good deal of pain, but as you continue to exercise, your wrist will become more limber and stronger and there will be no pain.

When you bend your left wrist, pour forth *Ki* through your left hand as in diagram 1-A, so that your *Ki* cannot be pushed back even when the right hand is bending that wrist. If your *Ki* returns to you as in diagram 1-B, then the practice is useless.

This *Nikyo* art can often be used to subdue an opponent when he seizes you by your lapel or chest.

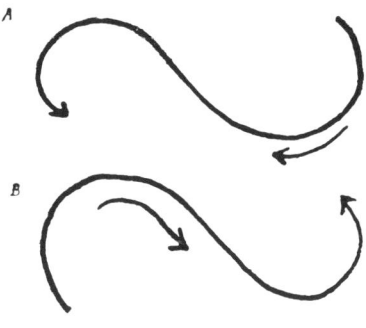

Diagram 1

9

2. Kote Gaeshi

Stand naturally as in *Nikyo*. At count One, bend your left wrist to the inside and with your right hand help to bend it even more.

The right hand must not mercy bend with the thumb. If the thumb does all the work, the shoulder is called upon to do too much. The little finger and ring finger oppose the thumb in grasping the wrist at the joint and a downward thrust with both hands natu-

10

rally gives greater strength to the thumb and makes it easier to bend the left wrist fully

This too is painful in the beginning but gradually strengthens that wrist. The *Kote-Gaeshi* art is used in throwing an opponent. Count Two, Three, Four and Five as in the *Nikyo* exercise.

Repeat with the right wrist.

3. Relax

Let both arms hang, completely limp, and shake your wrists and fingers rapidly. If strength is put into the fingers, it will be impossible to shake them rapidly. Make your one point the center of your thoughts and let the vibration from the wrists go through your whole body so that the whole body can relax. This exercise is done without counting. If you put tension into your body, you cannot move quickly; if you relax your muscles, you can move quickly but strength is lacking. Put your *Ki* on the one point and relax the rest of your body, and you will be able to feel power surging forth from your whole body.

While both arms are lowered, and someone takes one of your hands and pushes it upward toward your shoulder, does your arm bend at the elbow? Does your shoulder rise? If either of these things happens, it shows that you are not truly relaxed, that your *Ki* is not centered on the one point. If it were, nothing would feaze you.

4. Rowing Exercise

It is easy enough to keep your *Ki* on the one point while you are standing up straight. But when you move to the right or left, forward or backward, it becomes a bit difficult. It is necessary to keep practicing and training yourself so that you may move in any direction yet not lose the one point.

First, take a half step forward with your left foot.

I. At count One, push your hips forward as though to push your one point forward horizontally and thrust your arms forward forcefully, keeping the wrists bent. The upper body is kept vertical, bending neither forward nor backward. The arms are not thrust forward so much as brought forward with the feeling of extending *Ki* from the hips. The right leg should be stretched easily to the rear.

Test A. *The instructor stops you at position 1, and places his hand against your bent wrist and pushes it back toward your shoulder. If your Ki has been extended right up to the wrist and your* one point *remains unmoved, the instructor will not be able to push you backward.*

Test B. *Your instructor pushes your hips from behind. If you are in the correct position as in Test A, you will be very strong and will not be moved easily.*

II. At count Two, draw back your hips, at the same time pulling back your wrists to your hips. It should be a pulling back with the hips and not a pulling back with the arms. The right leg then is slightly bent and the left leg is straightened.

Test C. *As you stop, your instructor will push your shoulder from the front. If you are exercising correctly, you will not be moved.* With your left foot forward, count One, Two; One, Two, as you repeat the exercise, then with your right foot forward, repeat.

Bear in mind that this exercise is more for the hips than for the arms.

5. Shomen-Uchi Ikkyo (Ikkajo)

This exercise trains you in the basic movements of *Shomen-Uchi Ikkyo* in which your opponent tries to strike you on the forehead with his fist and you push his hand down and throw him. You must practice keeping your one point even when you raise your arms.

I. Take a half step forward with your left foot and at count One, with your fingers opened wide and strength on the edge of your hands, lift up your arms from your hips. The movement of your hips is the same as in Exercise No. 4.

Test A. *Your instructor pushes your wrists back toward your face. If you keep your one point and pour forth your Ki into infinity, you will be immovable.*

Test B. *Same as in Exercise 4.*

II. At count Two, bring your arms down to your hips, your hand forced into fists.
Test C. Same as Test C of Exercise No. 4.

You practice first with your left foot forward, then with your right foot forward. This will hold true of all the exercises to follow. To avoid repetition, let it be understood that what is done with the left is to be repeated with the right.

14 15

If you pour forth *Ki* at all times as you move your arms, centrifugal force tends to make them move in circular lines, your strength being on the periphery as it were. Testing by your instructor leaves you undaunted. Contrariwise, if your strength is in the inner side of your arms, your *Ki* is drawn inward and your posture is weak.

6. Zengo Undo

In Exercise No. 5, it is easy to keep your one point and pour forth *Ki* because you are required to face only one opponent. But the arts of *AIKIDO* may require you to deal with not only one opponent but many opponents simultaneously. You must practice so that you can meet instantly opponents attacking from any direction, front, back, left or right, keeping the one point at all times and always maintaining a posture of strength.

Both Exercise No. 6 and No. 7 *(Happo Undo)* are intended to prepare you in mind and body to move surely and quickly in any direction at any time anywhere.

I. Stand as at the beginning of Exercise No. 5.

63

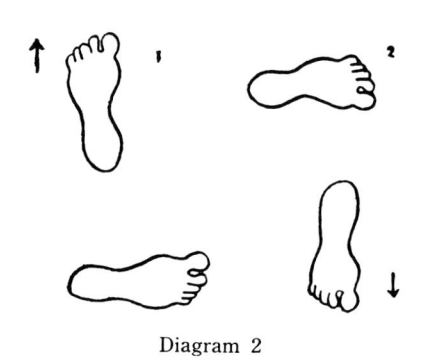

At counts One and Two, repeat the movements of Exercise No. 5 and with your fists at your hips turn your hips swiftly to the right on your toes and face the rear.

II. Naturally, when you turn to face your rear, your right foot will be in front. At counts Three and Four, do the same movement as at counts One and Two. At the end, you will be facing forward as at I.

As you turn your hips, maintain the one point. While you face forward, your *Ki* must be poured forth forward and when you face the rear, your *Ki* must go in the direction you are facing, not in the former direction. If this is not done, and your mind remains in the former direction, there is no coordination of mind and body, and a test by your instructor will show that your power has become very weak.

Diagram 2

7. Happo Undo

Count One. Do the same exercise as counts One and Two of Exercise No. 5 rapidly, hold your wrists at your hips, turn to the rear and wait for count Two. When you lift up your arms, step forward with your left foot and let the right foot follow.

Count Two. Repeat the same movement as at count One; turn to the rear and advance slightly.

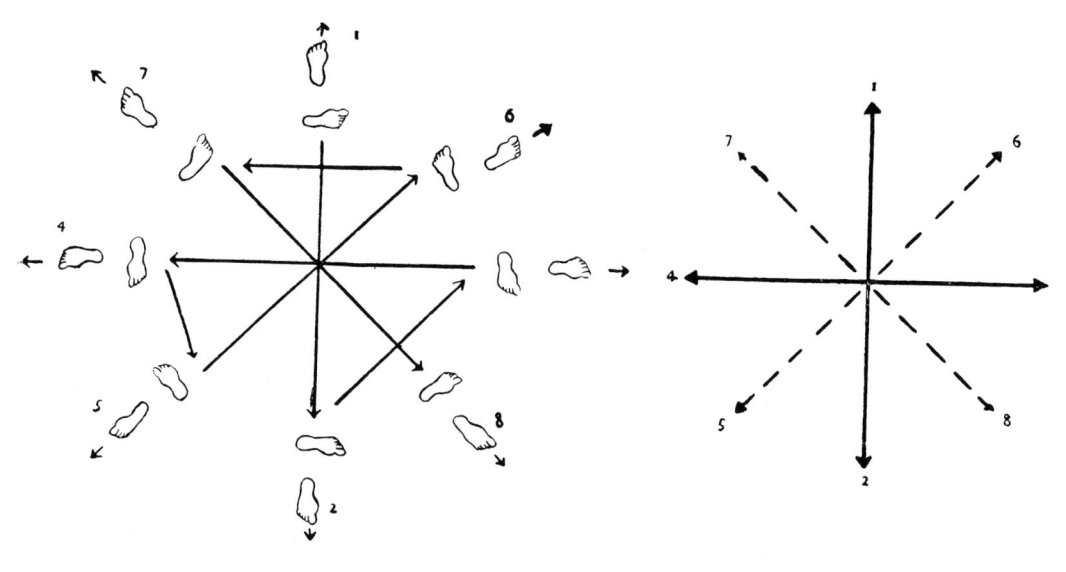

Diagram 3

Diagram 4

Count Three. Repeat the same movement as at count One; keep your right foot as it is, but take a step toward the left with your left foot.

Count Four. Repeat the same movement as at count One and turn to the rear.

Count Five. Repeat the same movement as at count One, the direction being halfway between Two and Four.

Count Six. The direction is between One and Three.

Count Seven. This is between One and Four.

Count Eight. This is between Two and Three.

Observe that those movements from Five to Eight are halfway between One to Four, and you learn then that *Happo Undo* means Eight-Direction Exercise.

Begin by practicing *Happo Undo* slowly and correctly and gradually increase your speed. It is most important to extend your whole mind in the same direction as that of your body movement. If your mind is delayed and separated from your body or if it keeps thinking only of your footwork, you will not be able to move smoothly and your power will be weakened.

As mind controls body, if you pour forth your *Ki* positively in any direction, your body will follow naturally.

8. Kokyuho Undo

This exercise corresponds to the *AIKIDO* art which shows how to lead an opponent by the correct timing of your movements.

16   17

Preparatory posture: the left foot a half step forward, the left hand stretched out, the wrist bent downward so that the fingers point backward toward the body (Photo 16).

18

19

20

21

Test A. The instructor pushes his hand against your bent wrist. Your elbow must not bend nor should your body move backward.

Test B. When the instructor pushes your hips from behind, you must remain unmoved as in tests in previous exercises.

At count One, keep your wrist as is but move your hips close to it (Photo 17), then turn your hips to the right, turn your face to the rear and with your right foot, take one step toward your own rear as in Photo 18.

Test C. Your instructor grasps your left wrist from behind and pulls it back. If you continue to keep your one point and pour forth Ki through your arm, your left arm will not be moved.

Count Two. Drop your left arm and stretch your right arm forward as in Photo 19, take a step forward with your right foot, bring your hips close to your right wrist, step backward with four left foot, your posture then being as in photo 20.

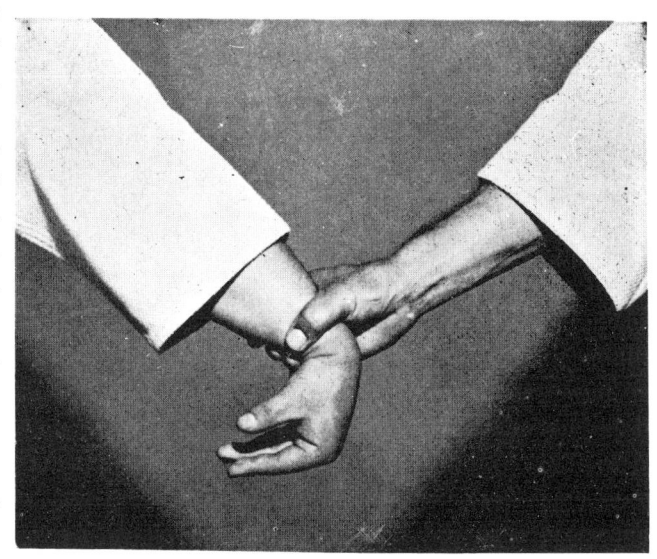

22

Count One. This time it will be the right foot forward and the right arm extended (Photo 21). At count Two, drop your right arm and stretch out your left arm, and so on.

This exercise is used to lead your opponent, not resisting him, when he seizes your wrist. As in Photo 22, his power will follow in the same direction as that of your fingers if you bend your wrist well and pour forth your *Ki*. As your hips approach your wrist and you turn your hips backward, his power always flows in the same direction as yours, so you are able to lead his power without resistance.

All methods in which one's movements are calculated to lead an opponent's power are called *Kokyuho* and when this law is used in throwing an opponent, that throw is called *Kokyu Nage*.

9-1. Tekubi Kosa Undo

Face the front and stand naturally with feet about two feet apart, shoulder relaxed, arms hanging loosely, drained of all strength, wrists fully bent. The weight of your arms comes down to the back of your hands and you will feel it there.

At count One, cross your hands in front of the one point, keeping your wrists bent and your arms relaxed (Photo 23). Then bring both arms back to the starting position.

Repeat this exercise five times with the left hand outside and then five times with the right hand outside.

Test A. Your instructor will have you halt when you have crossed your hands and push the back of your hands up toward your shoulder. As long as you concentrate on the one point and, relaxing your arms completely, feel their weight on the back of your hands, your instructor will not be able to move your arms upward, nor will he be able to move your body backward.

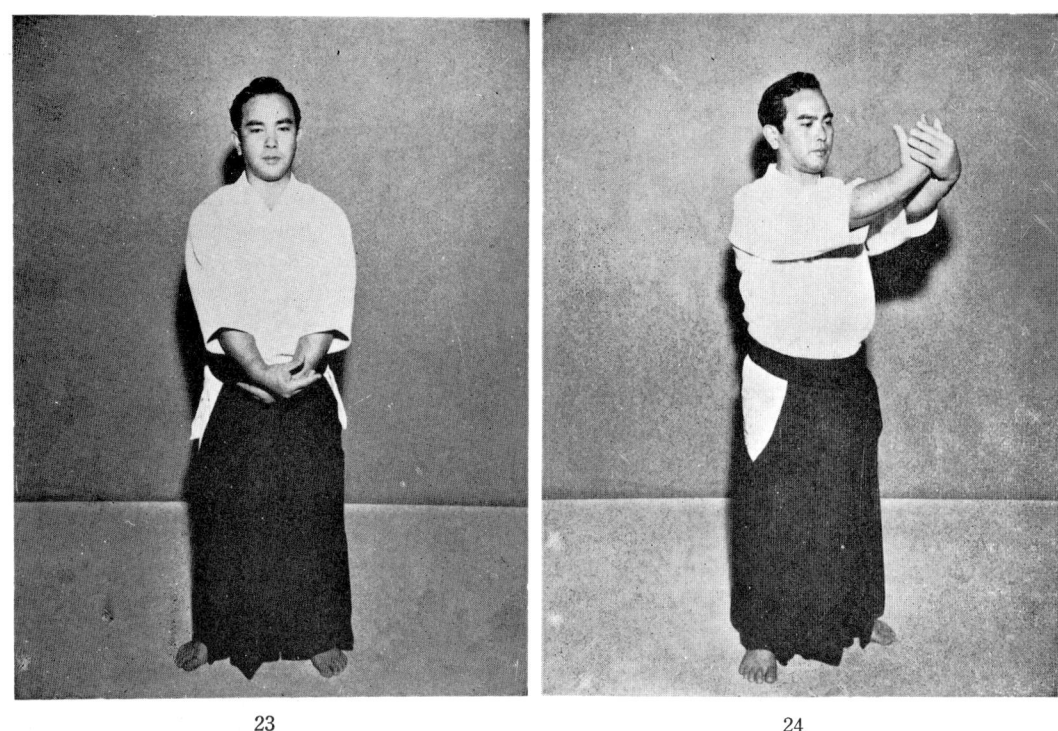

23   24

This exercise is used when some one seizes both of your hands. If you try to release them by force or to seize your opponent's hands, you will find it very difficult if he is a powerful man.

But if your movements correspond to the correct execution of this excercise, you can easily release yourself or seize your opponent's hands and throw him.

In other words, if you bend your wrist and let your *Ki* flow into the back of your hand, your opponent's *Ki* will follow in the same direction. Because you move in the same direction as your opponent, you move smoothly, but if you put strength into your arms, strength will clash with strength and your movements will not be smooth.

9-2. Tekubi Joho Kosa Undo

Stand as in *Tekubi Kosa* (Photo 24).

Count One. Instead of crossing your hands in front of you, swing your hands up and cross them in front of your forehead. Simply raise your hands; do not let your thought follow them. You must not lose the one point.

Test A. When you swing your arms up, your instructor will shove your hands toward your face. As long as you keep the one point and pour forth your Ki, you will not be moved.

10. Sayu Undo

Stand easily with feet apart.

Count One. Swing your arms up to the left side, palms upward, your face always to the front (Photo 25).

Count Two. Lower your hips by bending your left knee and straightening out your right leg. Keep your upper body erect (Photo 26).

Test A. If you lower your hips to the left, your instructor will shove you by your hips to the left. Keep the upper body upright and keep the one point, and you will not be

25   26

moved. *But if you incline your body to the left as in Photo 29, you will lose the one point and will be moved by the slightest shove.*

Test B. As you halt at the position assumed in Photo. 27, your instructor will push your arms up from below. If you have put strength into your arms, he will be able to lift them up easily but if you have drained the strength out of your arms and

69

you can feel their weight on the underside of your arms, he will not be able to lift them so easily.

27

28

29

Make a conscious effort to think about the underside of your arms. If your mind is on the upperside of the arms, they can be lifted up easily.

Count Three. Do the same movement toward your right side, completing it at count Four (Photos 27 and 28).

When you are doing this exercise, you must feel confident that you can throw your opponent by movements of your arms as at counts Two and Four.

If you try to throw him down using only your arms, you will find it difficult, but if you learn to use your hip movement to throw him, you will find it easy. If your arms and hips can be moved easily by your instructor's pushing, you cannot expect to throw an opponent.

11. Ude Furi Undo

30

31

Stand easily with feet apart.

Count One. Swing your arms to the left, pouring *Ki* outward and making a

32

33

circle with the finger tips (Photo 30). Count Two. Swing them to the right in the same manner (Photo 31).

Test A. As you swing your arms to the left, your instructor pushes you to the left by your hips. If you put strength into your arms or shoulders and lose the one point, he will move you easily. If you keep the one point and relax your arms and shoulders, he will have difficulty moving you.

Counts One and Two are to be repeated several times. Then the instructor will count One, Two, Three, Four. When next he says, "One," take a step forward with your right foot, turn your body to your left side and step backward with your left foot, always keeping time (Photo 32).

Test B. Though your instructor pushes your right shoulder, you should not move.

At count Two, swing both arms to the right, take a big step forward with your left foot, turn to your right side, take a backward step with your right foot and face the same direction as you did at count One (Photo 33). Repeat this several times.

34 35

If you can keep the one point at all times, in leaping about and stepping forward or backward for example, you will not make loud sounds with your feet. Begin this exercise slowly, then gradually increase your tempo.

The movements in this exercise are used often in *AIKIDO*.

The principle involved is the same as that of a spinning globe. No matter who your opponent may be, you can use the principle to suck him in and throw him at will. The one point becomes the center, your arms become the radius and the circles you make with your finger tips as you perform this exercise. If you draw your *Ki* inward or stop pouring forth *Ki*, the radius becomes loose and you cannot make the circle that is required.

12. Ushiro Tori Undo

Stand naturally with feet apart.

This exercise gives you practice in the movements used to throw an opponent forward when he sneaks up from behind you and pins both of your arms to your sides.

At count One, stretch your arms forward, at the same time taking a step forward with your left foot. Keep the one point and pour forth *Ki* in the direction of your fingers through the outside of your arms (Photo 34).

Test A. Your instructor will try to force your arms down to your body. But as long as you keep the one point and think of your power gushing out through your arms, he will not be able to do so.

At count Two, bend your left knee; then simultaneously as though flipping something over your head lower your left arm, raise your right arm, throw your upper body forward and straighten out your right leg (Photo 35). Next straighten up as you bring the left foot back to its original position and await count Three.

Test B. While you are still bending forward, your instructor will push you by your hips from behind. It will not do if you stagger forward. If you remember to relax your arms and keep the one point, your pose will be unshaken.

At counts Three and Four, repeat with your right foot stepping forward.

In Test A, if your arms can be forced down by your instructor's arms, you will not be able even to move forward. If your arms are not pressed down, you will be able to walk forward and throw your opponent forward.

When you are throwing him forward as in Photo 35, do not put his body on your hips but let him slide down by inclining your body forward. If you put his body on your hips, you will have his weight to bear and you will experience the difficulty of having to throw a heavy object. Instead, you use your arms and body to form a sort of chute for him to slide as you fling him and let him fly out.

13. Ushiro Tekubi Tori Zenshin Undo

Stand naturally with feet apart, keeping your wrists bent with fingers pointing forward (Photo 36).

Test. A. Your instructor will try to push your arm upward to test you.

At count One, take a step forward with your left foot, at the same time lifting your arms up to your forehead, always bending your wrists fully and pouring *Ki* out through the back of your hands (Photo 37).

As you lift up your arms, your fingers are pointing toward your face (Photo 38). Twist your wrists so that your fingers will point forward, then wait for count Two.

Test B. Your instructor will try to push your hands straight down. If you keep the one point and pour forth Ki out through the back of your hands, he will have diffi-

36

37

culty in doing this. But if you put strength into your arms, he will find it very easy to push your hands down.

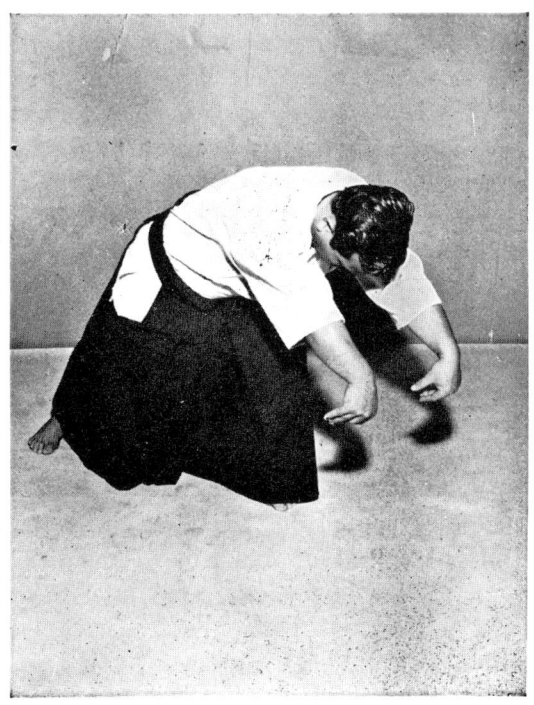

38

39

Count Two. Continue the momentum from count One and bend your body forward and get your hands down far enough, then return to the standing position, and wait for count Three (Photo 39).

Counts Three and Four. Do the same movements as at counts One and Two but step out with the right foot.

Test C. When you bend your body forward, your instructor will push you forward by your hips. If you keep the one point, relax your arms instead of putting strength into them, and pour forth Ki, he will not be able to shove you so easily.

The movements in this exercise are the same as those used to lead the opponent's hands and his *Ki* upward, and then throw him down when he grasps your wrists from behind.

If you do this exercise properly, you will know how to lead an opponent's hands, even though he may be a powerful man, but if you put strength into your arms and resist his power, you will not even be able to move your own hands.

14. Ushiro Tekubi Tori Kotai Undo

Stand naturally with feet apart.

Count One. Lift up your arms as in Exercise 13 and take a half step backward with your left foot. At this time, the weight of your body moves from the right foot to the left and you must keep a strong posture.

At count Two, take a big step backward with your right foot, and get your hands down forward, then return to the standing position.

Counts Three and Four. Do the same movements as at One and Two, but step out first with your right foot.

Test A. When you step backward, your instructor will push your hands back toward your body. Ki must be poured forth from your hands continuously because there is a tendency to pull Ki inward when one moves backward. As long as you keep your one point and pour forth Ki, you will not be moved.

This exercise gives practice in the movements for defending yourself when someone seizes both of your wrists from behind. After you step backward, there are many arts that can be used to throw him. If instead of your wrists your opponent seizes your shoulders, the same movement can be used.

15. Koho Tento (Koho Ukemi) Undo

Sit down on the floor. Put your left foot half forward and bend your right knee (Photo 40).

Count One. Without changing your posture, roll backward like a ball (Photo 41).

Count Two. Roll back to the starting position.

Test A. At the moment you return to the starting position, your instructor orders you to stop there and shoves your shoulders back with his hands. If you lose the one point and pull your Ki inward, you will fall back to the second position, but if you keep the one point and pour forth your Ki forward, you will remain in the starting position unmoved.

You must continue to pour forth *Ki* when you reach position three. Many students are inclined to let only their bodies advance to position three while their minds remain at position two.

Mind controls body. Your mind moves first and your body then follows.

If the mind is used correctly, you will not be moved even once in these tests, but if the mind is used incorrectly and left behind, you find yourself falling from the instructor's light shoving, no matter how strong you are or how much you practice. You must know how your mind works.

After you have practiced counts One and Two many times, your instructor orders you to stand up.

Now at count One, you fall to the floor, hips first so that you will fall like a rolling ball.

At count Two, you stand up again.

Test B. Just as you are about to stand up, your instructor will push you down with his hand by one shoulder. If your mind stops at the point where his hand touches you, you will not be able to rise but will drop to the floor again.

If you continue to extend your mind forward forcefully, you will be able to stand in spite of the interference.

In *AIKIDO* practice, very often you will drop or fall to the floor as in this exercise. Practice therefore falling smoothly without hitting your head or hips squarely on the mat. When you fall, do not hit the mat with your hand in order to soften the shock. If you are on a mat, you will not hurt yourself, but if you found it necessary to defend yourself on a concrete sidewalk, what then? If you are thrown too hard, make one roll with the throw and come to your feet. When you are to fall or be thrown, make youself round without any corners. If you have any corners, that is where you will be hit, but if you have no corners, there will be nowhere to be hit.

If in any of the tests, a slight shove is enough to make you fall, something is wrong. Your *Ki* should be so strong that when you rise, the one who shoves you is sent flying by your power.

42

16. Zenpo Kaiten (Zenpo Ukemi) Undo

As shown in Photo 42, assume a crouching position with your left foot forward, the back of your left hand on the mat before your left foot, and your hips low. Bend your head down, stretch the right arm over your head as though to protect it, with the wrist fully bent.

Then putting your head and right hand together between your left hand and foot, roll down forward, at the same time pushing your hips forward lightly. Bend your head fully, keeping in mind the admonition to make your body round (Photo 43).

After somersaulting thus once, do not stop but, with the momentum, continue to roll over again and again (Photos 44 and 45), making a circle around the room. At first, you become dizzy, but as you become accustomed to the exercise, that will pass. As you turn, always protect your head with your arms so that you will not hit the mat with your head.

43

When *AIKIDO Ukemi* is being done right, you will be round as a rolling ball, not even making a sound as you roll. When you are thrown down too hard, use that momentum to get up quickly. If when you are thrown on your side, you try to lessen the shock of your body's hitting the mat by striking the mat with your hand, you halt the momentum of your movements and abuse your body. If the base be concrete and not a springy mat, the *Ukemi* defense would then become impossible to apply. Practice until you are thoroughly familiar with *Ukemi*. Up to now, you have been doing what may be called "horizontal" exercises. Now you come to *Ukemi*, an exercise that you must practice until you are so proficient that you can perform it light-heartedly as a "vertical" exercise. *AIKIDO* is not a sport but a fighting art. If you make a mistake and fall, you remain calm and must be able to stand up instantly. If you are thrown in a real fight and think that you are defeated, you are really defeated. If you do not think so and stand up immediately, keeping your mind calm, you are not defeated, merely doing the vertical movement of your exercise.

44

I have divided the *AIKIDO* exercises into sixteen parts and explained them, but these are not all of the *AIKIDO* movements. In fact, there are several thousand arts in *AIKIDO* and we can make an exercise out of each one. Besides the sixteen, there are some others which two can practice together. For the benefit of beginners, I have mentioned in the foregoing pages only the typical, fundamental movements which are used most often in *AIKIDO* practice.

Even though a student has practiced *AIKIDO* for a long time, if he has done so without understanding the principles well, he must practice these exercises and submit to the tests in all humility to find out whether or not he is practicing correctly.

45

You cannot practice the real arts of *AIKIDO* by yourself but these exercises are designed for solo practice and will enable you to advance and gain strength if you practice them earnestly. An older man or a person who is physically weak should begin with these exercises only so that they do not strain themselves by throwing others or being thrown. Gradually mind and body will become strong and they will be able to practice all kinds of *AIKIDO* arts with much benefit to themselves.

If there are arts which you cannot seem to master, you may possibly have some mistaken notions about these arts. It will be wise then to practice the exercises connected with these arts and try to reason out the principles on which they are based and figure out how to use your mind and body correctly. You will be able to discover what you are doing wrong and correct yourself.

If you wish to advance more quickly than others, practice these exercise by yourself more sedulously than others, and change the contents of your subconscious mind so that you can use these arts in the right way without conscious thought.

EXPLANATION OF THE REAL ARTS OF AIKIDO

1. Fifty Arts

There are several thousand kinds of arts in *AIKIDO* and it will be impossible even to enumerate them here.

Why so many? If you are attacked by one man, or by two or more, in each case there is a different defense art suitable for such attacks. Whether or not your opponent has a weapon, and whether or not you yourself have a weapon naturally makes a difference in the arts you can apply. When an opponent grabs you by the hand or your shoulder, strikes at your face or the side of your face, or punches you on your chest, each will call for different defense tactics. When you are attacked from the front or from behind calls for the application of different arts.

There are many ways of attacking you and in order to cope with these there are more than ten defense arts for each such attack method.

In daily practice, you must learn first to move your body correctly. After you comprehend these movements, in a showdown in real life, if you have a stick, you must make use of it; if you have a sword, you should be able to use it. Anything that comes to hand can be used as a weapon, using its strong points. This is *AIKIDO*.

In sports, there are many rules and regulations as to certain places of your body that are not to be hit, holds that are barred, certain methods, like kicking and eye-gouging, that are not allowed, and so on. As a result of such agreements, the number of arts you need to learn are limited.

But in a real rough-and-tumble battle, though your opponents attack you in any way they choose, you cannot complain about it but must meet any attack. No holds are barred. You can understand then why there are several thousand kinds of arts in *AIKIDO*.

You do not need to learn all of them, of course. It will be enough for you to practice the fundamental arts of *AIKIDO* and learn how to use your mind and body together correctly. You can apply them to many other arts by yourself.

I have chosen the fifty most frequently used arts in daily practice and I will explain them in detail.

It is important for you to practice them thoroughly one by one and learn how to do them correctly. If you understand them only on the level of the conscious mind, they will not serve you in a real fight. You must practice them repeatedly again and again and yet again until you can use them without conscious thought.

If you learn these fifty arts well enough, you can learn another three hundred or five hundred by combining these fifty.

However, to learn many arts is not so important as to understand the principles underlying each art. Determine now to make a real effort first to do this.

Methods of Attack by Opponent	Techniques to be Applied	Variation
Katate-Tori	*Ikkyo*	*Irimi*
Kata-Tori	*Nikyo*	*Tenkan*
Yokomen-Uchi	*Sankyo*	
Shomen-Uchi	*Shiho-Nage*	
Mune-Tsuki	*Kote-Gaeshi*	
Katate-Tori Ryote-Mochi	*Kokyu-Nage*	
Ushiro Tekubi-Tori	*Kaiten-Nage*	
Ushiro Hiji-Tori		
Ushiro Kata-Tori		
Ushiro Kubi-Shime		
Ushiro-Tori		
Ushiro Katate-Tori Kubi-Shime		

The left column names the methods of attack by your opponent, the middle column, the arts or techniques to be applied to such attacks. Each of these arts can be applied in two ways, *Irimi* or *Tenkan*.

These two variations will be explained in the following chapter.

No. 1. *Katate-Tori Kokyu-Ho*   Tenkan
No. 2. *Katate-Tori Kokyu-Ho*   Irimi
No. 3. *Katate-Tori Kokyu-Nage*   (opposite side)
No. 4. *Katate-Tori Kote-Gaeshi*   (opposite side)
No. 5. *Kokyu-Dosa*
No. 6. *Katate-Tori Kokyu-Nage*
No. 7. *Katate-Tori Kote-Gaeshi*
No. 8. *Katate-Tori Kokyu-Nage*   Irimi (Ten-Chi)
No. 9. *Katate-Tori Kokyu-Nage*   Tenkan

No. 10.   *Katate-Tori Kokyu-Nage   Tenkan   (Katate-Tori Kaiten-Naeg)*
No. 11.   *Kata-Tori Ikkyo   Irimi*
No. 12.   *Kata-Tori Ikkyo   Tenkan*
No. 13.   *Kata-Tori Nikyo   Irimi*
No. 14.   *Kata-Tori Nikyo   Tenkan*
No. 15.   *Kata-Tori Kokyu-Nage   Irimi*
No. 16.   *Kata-Tori Kokyu-Nage   Tenkan*
No. 17.   *Yokomen-Uchi Shiho-Nage*
No. 18.   *Yokomen-Uchi Kokyu-Nage   Tenkan (A)*
No. 19.   *Yokomen-Uchi Kokyu-Nage   Tenkan (B)*
No. 20.   *Yokomen-Uchi Kokyu-Nage   Tenkan (C)*
No. 21.   *Yokomen-Uchi Kokyu-Nage   Irimi (A)*
No. 22.   *Yokomen-Uchi Kokyu-Nage   Irimi (B)*
No. 23.   *Shomen-Uchi Kokyu-Nage   Irimi*
No. 24.   *Shomen-Uchi Kote-Gaeshi*
No. 25.   *Shomen-Uchi Ikkyo   Irimi*
No. 26.   *Shomen-Uchi Ikkyo   Tenkan*
No. 27.   *Shomen-Uchi Nikyo   Irimi*
No. 28.   *Shomen-Uchi Nikyo   Tenkan*
No. 29.   *Shomen-Uchi Sankyo   Irimi*
No. 30.   *Shomen-Uchi Sankyo   Tenkan*
No. 31.   *Mune-Tsuki Kote-Gaeshi*
No. 32.   *Mune-Tsuki Kaiten-Nage*
No. 33.   *Mune-Tsuki Nikyo   Hantai Tenkan*
No. 34.   *Mune-Tsuki Kote-Gaeshi   Hantai Tenkan*
No. 35.   *Katate-Tori Ryote-Mochi Kokyu-Nage   Irimi*
No. 36.   *Katate-Tori Ryote-Mochi Kokyu-Nage   Tenkan (A)*
No. 37.   *Katate-Tori Ryote-Mochi Kokyu-Nage   Tenkan (B)*
No. 38.   *Katate-Tori Ryote-Mochi Kote-Gaeshi*
No. 39.   *Katate-Tori Ryote-Mochi Nikyo (1) (2)*
No. 40.   *Ushiro Tekubi-Tori   Ikkyo*
No. 41.   *Ushiro Tekubi-Tori   Kote-Gaeshi*
No. 42.   *Ushiro Tekubi-Tori   Sankyo*
No. 43.   *Ushiro Tekubi-Tori Kote-Gaeshi   Tenkan*
No. 44.   *Ushiro Hiji-Tori Kote-Gaeshi*
No. 45.   *Ushiro Kata-Tori Kote-Gaeshi*
No. 46.   *Ushiro Kata-Tori Kokyu-Nage   Tenkan (1)   Ago-tsukiage (2)*
No. 47.   *Ushiro Kubi-Shime Kokyu-Nage*
No. 48.   *Ushiro-Tori Kokyu-Nage*
No. 49.   *Ushiro Katate-Tori Kubi-Shime Sankyo*
No. 50.   *Ushiro Katate-Tori Kubi-Shime Sankyo*

2. The Words Most Frequently Used In AIKIDO
A. *Ki*

The word most frequently used in *AIKIDO* is *Ki*. *Ki* is a very convenient word because it has both a deep meaning connected with nature and a light meaning which is used in daily life. It is very difficult to define *Ki* and even more difficult to translate it into English. Therefore, the word *Ki* will be used in the explanation of *AIKIDO*.

In oriental thought, it is said that in the beginning there was chaos. The dust of chaos settled gradually to form the sun, the earth, the moon and the stars. On the earth, the elements combined to become minerals, animal and vegetable life. We call the chaotic condition before the universe took shape *Ki*. We say therefore, that all things came from *Ki*.

Ki itself has neither beginning nor end, nor increase nor decrease. Though its shape was changed, *Ki* itself was never changed. We can see many things around us, all made from *Ki*, and when they lose their shape, their elements return to *Ki*. Depending on what you believe, you call it God, or Buddha or Akua or some other name.

AIKIDO is the way of at-one-ment with cosmic power or *Ki*.

That is the deep meaning of *Ki*.

What is the light meaning of *Ki* used in our daily life? A good feeling, a bad feeling, a great feeling, timidity, vigor, courage, a retiring disposition, et cetera—these are terms used in our daily life. In each word or phrase, the Japanese use *Ki* as an integral part. The reason is that a human being was created from *Ki* of the universe. While he receives *Ki*, he is alive. Deprive him of *Ki* and he dies; he loses his human shape. So long as his body is filled with *Ki* and it pours forth abundantly, he is vigorous and filled with courage. On the contrary, when his body has run out of *Ki*, he is weak, cowardly and retiring.

In *AIKIDO* training, we make every effort to learn to fill our body with *Ki* and use it powerfully. Therefore, we must understand well the deep meaning of *Ki*.

(1) *Ki Wo Neru*—to train your *Ki*

The meaning of training your *Ki* is that you believe that your body is filled with *Ki* of the universe so you keep the one point, make it the center of your body and pour forth *Ki* from your whole body. You must train it in every movement of the *AIKIDO* arts.

(2) *Ki Wo Totonoeru*—To prepare your *Ki*

You keep your mind at the one point, let your breathing be calm and keep yourself calm, ready to move quickly at any time.

(3) *Ki Wo Dasu*—To pour forth *Ki*

Like an unbendable arm, if you think that your power is gushing out through your arm, it becomes very strong and difficult to bend. Such use of the mind is called pouring forth *Ki*.

If you believe that your *Ki* is gushing forth, your *Ki* is really gushing out. For example, as you are walking along and someone pushes you by your shoulder. If you pull your *Ki* inward or your mind trails behind your body, your attacker will be able to push you back or throw you down. If you pour forth your *Ki* and your mind is ahead of your body, he will not be able to push you back, but instead he himself will be pushed back by the impact.

Let us say there is clear water gushing out from a spring in a muddy stream. As long as this water gushes out, muddy water cannot get into the spring. But if the clear water stops flowing for even a moment, muddy water will enter the spring immediately.

Ki is like this spring water. As long as your *Ki* is being poured forth, your opponent's *Ki* does not come upon you. Stop pouring forth your *Ki* or pull your *Ki* inward and your opponent's power will engage you instantly.

If you would gain true understanding, you must practice diligently the art of pouring forth a constant stream of *Ki*. Master this and you will be able to see whether or not your opponent pours out his *Ki* merely by looking at his form and posture.

The power which is not directed against you is nothing for you to worry about, though it may be very strong. If you would understand non-resistance or non-aggression, the essential principle of *AIKIDO*, you must first practice pouring forth your *Ki*.

The reasoning back of non-resistance is not to run away from your opponent's strength but so to maneuver that his *Ki* does not engage you; make him lose his aggressive urge. This is the real victory. You may fell your opponent but as long as you leave him with the urge to attack, there may come a day when you will be defeated by him. The real victory comes when you expunge from his mind this urge to attack.

(4) *Ki No Nagare*—The stream of *Ki*

Whenever you keep pouring forth your *Ki* and swinging your arms, you draw a circle or a line that resembles a continuous stream of water. Such a stream is called "the stream of *Ki*."

If you set a point on the ground and use a length or rope as your radius, you can make a circle. Of course, the rope must be held taut or the circle will not be perfect. If you continuously pour forth your *Ki* and keep the one point, your hands will naturally move in a circle. If your *Ki* is poured forth sporadically, your form becomes ragged and you lose power. Then you move your body, as you move your one point too, your hands make eccentric circles and revolutions. Like diagram 5-a, b, and c, your stream can take many shapes and you can whirl your opponent into the strong stream of your *Ki* and throw him.

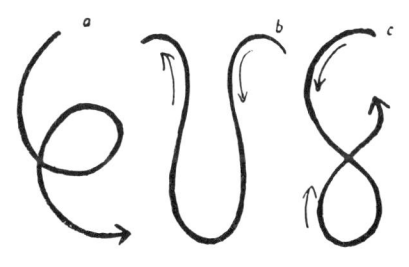

Diagram 5

(5) *Ki Wo Kiru*—To cut *Ki*

To cut *Ki* means to cut the stream of *Ki*. If your mind becomes frozen or you pull your *Ki* inward for even a moment, your stream of *Ki* is cut off and its power will likewise be cut off.

As an analogy, once you start pushing a cart, momentum keeps it going with not too much effort on your part. If you stop, you must fight inertia to get it moving again.

If you continue the stream of *Ki* and do not cut it, you can lead your opponent by bringing him into your stream of *Ki* and letting his power go back against himself, so that throwing him down will be quite easy.

When you cut your *Ki* at any time, his *Ki* will come upon you immediately and you will not be able to move him, You must practice always not to cut your *Ki* but to continue to pour it forth.

(6) *Ki Ga Nukeru*—To lose *Ki*

To lose *Ki* means that you have forgotten your one point and are in no condition to pour forth your *Ki*. When you are discouraged or tired of your work, put the cause down as loss of *Ki*.

You will never succeed in anything if you lose your *Ki*. Especially since *AIKIDO* is the training of *Ki*, it is better to stop practicing if you are doing it without *Ki* because that will cause you to form bad habits. You must always put your *Ki* into your training.

B. *Kokyu*

The words *Kokyu Ho* and *Kokyu Nage* are used very often in *AIKIDO*. There are many kinds of arts especially in *Kokyu Nage*, with numerous movements and variation of these for each *Kokyu Nage* art.

Kokyu is, in plain words, the movement of your *Ki* or the movement of your body following *Ki*.

If you have strong *Kokyu*, your body is filled with powerful *Ki* and you are moving and throwing your opponent correctly. In other forms of *Budo*, or the martial arts, the phrase "strong power" is used, but in *AIKIDO*, we say strong *Kokyu* because the arts of *AIKIDO* are concerned not only with physical matters but also with *Ki*. *Kokyu Ho* is the way that leads others by *Kokyu*, and *Kokyu Nage* is the art of throwing others by *Kokyu*.

C. *Hanmi*

Always face your opponent in the posture of *Hanmi*. If you stand before him, keeping your feet together, your mind will be fixed there and you will have difficulty in moving when he attacks you. To stand with your left foot a half step forward is called Left *Hanmi* and with your right foot a half step forward, Right *Hanmi*.

The stance keeps you strong in the rear yet you can move swiftly at will by using both feet, each one acting in concert with the other. With this stance you do not put the center of gravity of your body on one leg only but on your one point and you must stand as though by mind and not by your legs, so that you can defend yourself against any attack by your opponent.

D. *Ma-Ai*

In a real fight, the distance between you and your opponent is important. If you approach too close, you connot maneuver in avoiding a sudden attack. If on the other hand you keep yourself too far from him, it will be difficult for you to use the arts against him. You must keep a proper distance, not too close nor too far away from him. To keep the proper distance between you and your opponent is called taking *Ma-ai*.

If you always pour forth your *Ki*, you will understand naturally how to take *Ma-ai* according to the height of your body. If you pull your *Ki* inward, you will lose the *Ma-ai*. It is by forgetting to take *Ma-ai* that some one will stick his neck out, so to speak, and get his block knocked off.

The distance from which your opponent must take one step forward to attack you and from which you must take one step forward to attack him is generally considered good *Ma-ai*.

When you are closer than this *Ma-ai*, you must already be holding him down.

E. *Orenai Te*—Unbendable arm

It is called Unbendable Arm when you pour forth your *Ki* through it and it is difficult to bend even though you do not put any strength into it.

Nobody can put strength into his arm constantly. If you are strong only while you put forth strength, it will be useless when something suddenly happens about you.

Be relaxed at all times and still strong at any time you choose. Unbendable Arm does not depend on the angle of the arm. If you continue to pour out your *Ki*, your arm is always unbendable.

F. *Fudo No Shisei*—Immovable posture

Immovable posture does not mean one from which you cannot move easily but one in which you keep your mind on the one point, relax the rest of your body and fill it with *Ki*. It means the posture in which your mind is not disturbed by anything; neither is your body moved. When you do move, your mind and body must move in coordination.

G. *Irimi*

When your opponent's power is coming toward you and yours against his, there will be a head-on collision and the stronger will win. *Irimi* is the way to advance toward your opponent, not meeting him with resistance but leading his power at will. To understand *Irimi*, you must keep your one point and Unbendable Arm or you cannot make *Irimi* work for you. *Irimi* is the special art found only in *AIKIDO*.

It enables you to demonstrate directly the principle of the art of non-resistance, letting your opponent's power return to himself no matter how powerful he may be.

H. *Tenkan*

Tenkan is the way to lead your opponent's power without stopping it, by turning your body when his power is coming toward you. In *Irimi*, you must sometimes move in a strong, straight line, but in *Tenkan*, you must always move in a strong circular movement or revolution. You can suck in an opponent's power into your *Tenkan* movement and let his power dissipate itself so that you can subsequently lead him to fall down.

Almost all of the *AIKIDO* arts are used on both *Irimi* and *Tenkan*.

I. *Nage*

Nage is the one who is attacked by his opponent and throws him down.

J. *Uke*

Uke is the one who attacks the other and is thrown down by him.

EXPLANATION OF ARTS OF TECHNIQUES

No. 1. Katate-Tori Kokyu-Ho Tenkan

Nage: Against *Uke*, *Nage* stands in the position of left *Hanmi*, and extends the left arm with wrist bent downward, fingers pointed toward himself, and the back of the hand thrust toward *Uke*, and lets him grasp his wrist. This posture is the same as in Exercise No. 8.

Uke: Stands in the position of right *Hanmi* and grasps the left wrist of *Nage* (Photo 46).

Nage: Bends his wrist, pours forth his *Ki* and, while keeping the back of the hand extended, brings his hips close to his wrist (Photo 47). He continues turning his hips to the right until he has changed direction, and steps back with his right foot (Photo 48). At this time, he and *Uke* are both facing in the same direction although back to back.

Photo 46: Even if *Nage* tries forcibly

to pull away his wrist from *Uke*'s grasp, he will not find it easy. *Uke*'s *Ki* is poured forth toward *Nage* and in addition his fingers are locked around his wrist so that the use of force alone will not effect a release. However, if *Nage* bends his wrist and pours forth his *Ki*, his *Ki* will flow in the same direction as *Uke*'s.

Photo 47: If *Nage* tries to pull his left hand toward himself, he will collide with *Uke*'s *Ki* and force. From *Nage*'s standpoint, the difficulty is that to pull his wrist toward himself means a retreat for his own *Ki*. He should push his hips forward and advance.

Photo 48: If *Nage* turns in the same direction as *Uke*, he will be moving in exactly the same direction as *Uke*. As he pivots on his hips and turns to the right, *Uke* naturally follows.

In this instance, *Nage*'s *Ki* in the beginning faces *Uke*'s *Ki* but when *Nage* pivots and turns his body around, his *Ki* changes direction with his finger tips; then in other words, they point in a direction opposite to that at the beginning. Otherwise, *Nage*'s hand may be pulled back by *Uke*.

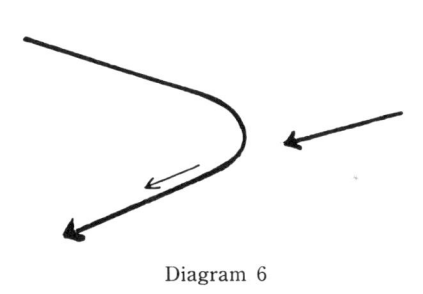

Diagram 6

This movement is an exercise for turning not only the body but also the mind and must have a forward look. When the face is turned around, the mind must make a complete turn-around. Even if *Nage*'s hand is held by his opponent or *Nage* has moved to place *Uke* behind him, he must not let his mind stay behind. This movement should be practiced repeatedly until you have learned to change your mind at will, and you will find this ability important in your daily life as well.

For example, you may feel angry in the morning, and continue to feel angry all day because your mind is set. But once you realize that you should not be angry, you must be able to change the direction of your mind immediately. Or if the cause of your anger is gone, you must at once stop being angry. Any one who continues to be angry after the cause is gone has let his mind stay behind. There may be some persons who enjoy being angry, but the rest of us should remember that it takes three times more energy to scowl than to smile.

To enjoy life, let us cut off from our conscious mind all evil and injurious thoughts, and keep whatever is pleasant and enjoyable.

In *AIKIDO*, you will learn that to think of one opponent only may mean that the next opponent will be able to hit you. Change your mind from moment to moment and you will be able to face each opponent more successfully.

Kokyu-Ho is the basic movement in learning this principle. Practice it assiduously until it becomes second nature with you.

Practice alternately with the left hand and the right hand, and learn the principle of not resisting your opponent's strength nor trying to stop him but using his own strength to lead him.

No. 2. Katate-Tori Kokyu-Ho Irimi

Uke: Same as No 1. Grasps the left wrist of *Nage* with his right hand (Photo 49).

Nage: If he tries to advance toward *Uke* from this hold, he will find it difficult because *Uke* is holding his wrist too tightly for him to do so.

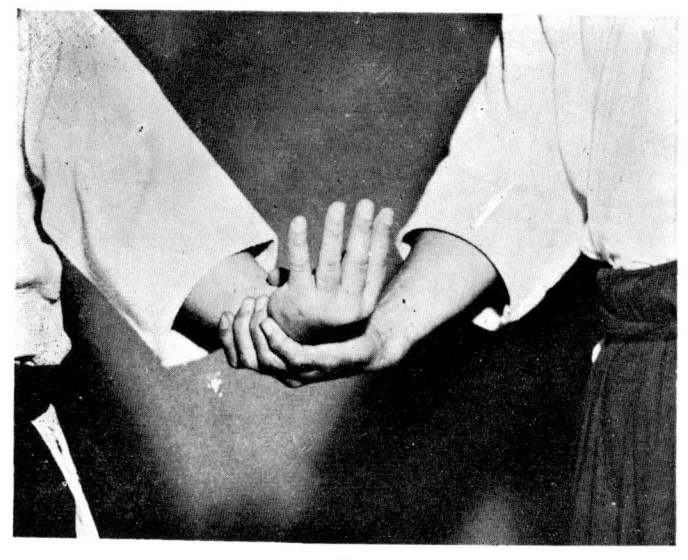

With immovable posture coupled with unbendable arm, *Nage* calmly turns his wrist so that his palm faces upward and, pointing his fingers upward, thrusts out the back of his hand. When *Nage* does this, his *Ki* flows through his finger tips, paralleling *Uke*'s forward-and-upward movement.

Next, without moving the wrist, *Nage* steps smoothly with the left foot to a position in front of *Uke* then pulls up the right foot. This must be accomplished while keeping hip movement to a horizontal line without any vertical motion (Photo 50).

49

50

51

Nage's wrist, making use of *Uke's* force, moves upward along the line of least resistance. As *Uke* follows along, he loses his balance. If *Uke* tries to pull *Nage's* arm down by force, do not let him do so.

If *Nage* extends his left arm and left foot and does not pull up his right foot, as shown in Photo 51, one point of balance is lost and *Uke* finds it easy to pull *Nage's* arm down, this in turn creating an opportunity for him to throw *Nage*. This is an illustration of how not to do it.

This movement should be practiced repeatedly, beginning alternately with the right arm and left arm.

Important Note: In progressing from his position in Photo 49 to Photo 50, if *Nage* puts strength into his arm, it will only telegraph his intention and he will be stopped by *Uke*.

Nage must practice so that the instant *Uke* grasps his wrist he can advance smoothly. He must keep in mind that he is not raising his arm. As he advances his hips, his arm rises naturally.

If *Nage* tries to raise his arm, he will clash with *Uke's* force. Without adding force to the arm, advancing the hips without force, using *Uke's* force on himself—this is the principle of *Irimi*. It is by learning this movement that the basic principle can be grasped.

No. 3. Katate-Tori Kokyu-Nage (Opposite Side)

Uke: Grasps *Nage's* right wrist with the right hand.

Nage: Without putting strength into the arm that has been grasped or resisting the strength of *Uke*, *Nage* pours forth *Ki*, remaining always at ease (Photo 52). It is easier to pour forth *Ki* if the fingers of the hand are widely separated.

The left hand must also pour forth *Ki*. Keeping the one point as the center, *Nage* leaps to the right rear of *Uke* and pushes him down by his neck completely but gently (Photo 53).

As the left foot was used in leaping without losing momentum, *Nage* turns his body to the right and steps forward with the right foot (Photo 54).

The movements up to this point are exactly the same as in Exercise 11, *Ude-Furi Undo*.

Uke having his neck pushed downward, tries unconsciously to push it upward. *Nage* grasps this opportunity and encircles *Uke's* neck with his right arm, his left hand

53

54

55

56

still pushing *Uke's* neck down, and turns *Uke's* throat upward (Photo 55). As *Uke* loses his balance, *Nage* steps forward with his right foot, sending *Ki* to his hips, and throws

Uke, his arms moving as though he were trying to thrust his fingers into the earth (Photo 56).

Photo 52: Even if *Uke* pushes back *Nage's* arm, it will not do for *Nage* to let his shoulder go up. If *Uke* pulls *Nage's* arm, *Nage* should follow and with the momentum leap in. *Ki* must be kept constantly concentrated on the one point and the body relaxed so that it will be easy to take advantage of *Uke's* force and leap in.

Photo 53: *Nage* stretches his right hand toward the same direction that *Uke's* arm points. If *Nage* tries to change direction forcibly, he will clash with *Uke's* force. *Nage* should also push down with his left hand in the direction that *Uke's* Ki moves: that is, in the direction that *Uke's* arm points.

Photo 54: To press down on the neck and then when your opponent pushes back, to use that momentum to throw him backward is to use the principle of the swing, or pendulum. The swing will go as far as it can and then swing back again. Try to stop it in mid-swing and you are clashing with a great force. Throw a rubber ball on the ground with great force: it will rebound with great force. In the same way, the harder *Nage* presses with his left hand on *Uke's* neck, the greater will be *Uke's* reaction and the easier it will be to push his head back with the right arm.

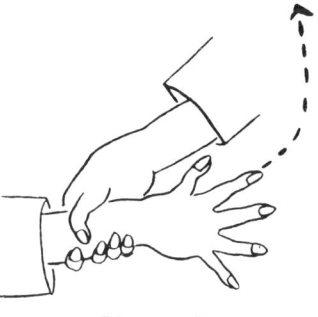

Diagram 7

Nage should help *Uke* to go along the direction of his *Ki*. When he discovers that he has gone too far and wants to return, let him return. It is with this lighter feeling that these movements should be performed.

Nage raises the right arm in a curving upward motion. If the right arm is merely pushed back against *Uke's* right arm, there is a collision of two forces and raising the arm becomes very difficult. The right arm should be raised while pouring forth *Ki* as shown in the diagram above so that *Uke's* right arm automatically follows and is raised up. *Nage's* Ki must be poured forth along the side of the small finger.

The right arm and the hips must be lowered completely, and when standing up, the arm must be positioned as shown in the illustration. Then *Ki* is poured forth and *Nage* stands up.

Photo 55: Do not work to throw *Uke's* body. Lead *Uke's* mind backward, and he will automatically fall.

The right arm goes up with the finger tips first and encircles *Uke's* neck. Then with the finger tips pointing to the ground, *Nage* throws *Uke* as though he were dropping him off his finger tips.

When *Nage* encircles *Uke's* neck with his arm, he does not hit his throat with his arm. If *Nage* imagines that his rigid arm is round and truly wraps it around *Uke's* neck, he can throw *Uke* with ease.

Photo 56: After throwing *Uke*, it will not do for *Nage* to let *Ki* out of the body or to let his guard down. He must always imagine that enemies are around and prepare to defend himself against the next attack from any quarter.

No. 4. Katate-Tori Kote-Gaeshi (Opposite Side)

Nage: In the same manner as in No. 3, *Nage* leaps to a position behind *Uke* (Photo 54). But after that, he does not touch *Uke*'s neck but *Uke*'s right wrist.

Then he grasps *Uke*'s wrist from the thumb side in such a way that his thumb is on the back of *Uke*'s hand and the four fingers are on the side of his palm.

When *Nage* leaps in, his momentum must be great enough to cause *Uke*'s body to follow and turn with him, constantly keeping *Uke*'s arm extended as he turns (Photo 58).

With the left hand, *Nage* bends back *Uke*'s right wrist (as in Excercise 2), and places the right palm on *Nage*'s own left thumb. (The right wrist that *Uke* was holding becomes automatically freed as *Nage* leaps in). When *Uke*'s wrist is pressed downward with both hands, *Uke* is overturned (Photo 59).

Keeping the left hand as is, *Nage* places his right hand to *Uke's* elbow and walks around his head. *Uke* turns, facing downward.

Nage holds *Uke's* wrist between his body and left elbow and bending *Uke's* left elbow with the right arm, pushes him tightly against his own chest. *Nage* turns and twists his upper body toward *Uke's* head and *Uke* will give up (Photo 60). In Excercise 2, you practice bending your own wrist, but in an actual match, *Nage* bends *Uke's* wrist. When bending the wrist, do so with the smallest possible angle as though trying to roll *Uke's* finger tips into the palm (Photo 62).

If *Uke* puts strength into his fist, his *Ki* runs through to the center and it will be difficult to bend it forcibly. Do not even think of bending his wrist. Since *Uke's Ki* follows the clenched fingers and continues into the center of his fist, do not try to stop this *Ki* but try rather to extend it by rolling this *Ki* to the center of *Uke's* fist. Then no matter how much strength *Uke* puts into his fist, his wrist can be bent very easily.

Merely learning the form of *AIKIDO* will not give you the ability to make practical use of it. A good example is the *Kote-Gaeshi*. Learn the importance of the rules of *Ki;* do not clash with your opponent's *Ki*, but apply techniques that will extend it, so that your opponent will gladly follow your lead. If you do not understand the principles of *Ki* and your opponent is stronger than you are, you will not be able to apply your technique at all. Since mind controls the body, it is essential to learn first to lead the mind.

Photo 60: When you are bending *Uke's* arm, do not try to bend the joint against the

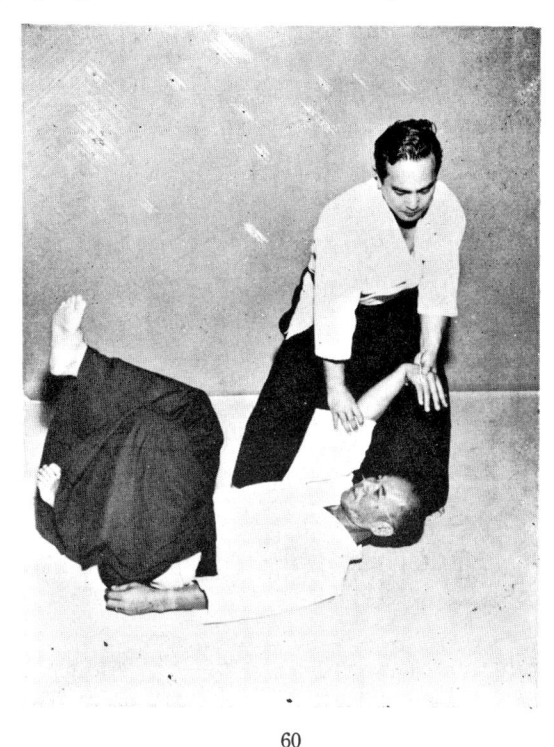

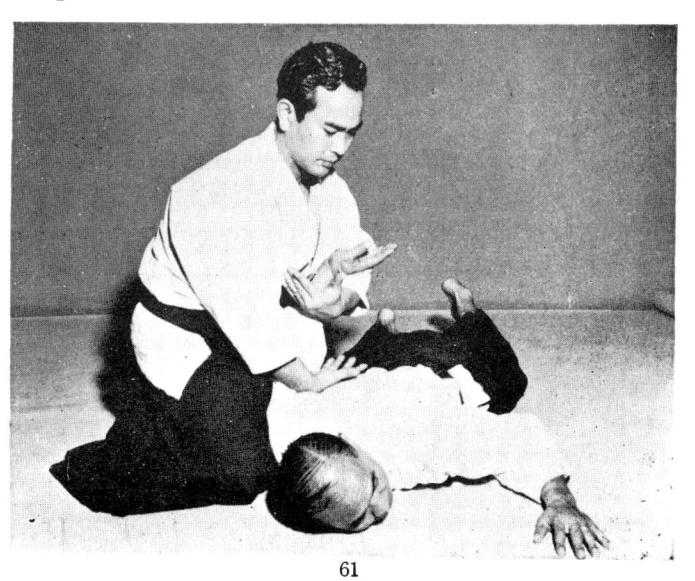

60

61

93

natural direction in which it bends. Always bend the arm at the elbow, as though making a circle. If done properly, it will not do violence to the body and only a little strength is needed to make your opponent surrender.

In holding down an opponent in *AIKIDO*, always make him face downward. In this position, you can control him as long as you have even one arm under control (Photo 61). If he is facing upward, he can use his arms and legs, and it is very difficult to control him. This is true especially if *Uke* can catch *Nage* from below, and *Uke's* companions attack *Nage*. *Nage* can do nothing to defend himself. Hold your opponent face down, and if need arises, be in a position to take on the next opponent at any time.

People seeing one man bending the wrist of another say, "*Gyaku-Te*" or "*Gyaku*," but *AIKIDO* does not use *Gyaku-Te*. *Gyaku* refers to anything that is opposed to the principles of Nature; while *Jun* refers to anything that follows the principles of Nature. *AIKIDO* follows the rules of Nature, bends as Nature orders it to bend, falls as Nature orders it to fall, leads an opponent in the direction of his *Ki*, and is therefore *Jun*. *Nikyo*, which will be explained later on in this book, is often mistaken for *Gyaku-Te*, but here too the bending is according to Nature's laws.

62

To bend any joint forcibly in the direction that Nature never intended it to be bent is *Gyaku* and will do violence to the body. All *AIKIDO* techniques benefit the health and all *AIKIDO* students will realize, as they practice, that this is true.

Generally speaking, to learn *Gyaku* in order to injure others manifests an undesirable attitude. To learn the principles of Nature and to practice them openly is *AIKIDO*. As one improves oneself, so acting toward one's opponent that his health is benefited, and both advance together—that is the attitude toward learning that is desirable and hereby recommended.

No. 5. Kokyu-Dosa

Kokyu-Dosa must be practiced every day at the end of the regular practice. This is fundamental, involving as it does the determination of a point about two inches below the navel as the generating center of powerful *Ki*.

There are many kinds of *Kokyu-Dosa*, but the one explained here is typical.

Practice it assiduously and learn how to throw an opponent not by brute strength but by the use of *Ki*.

Both *Nage* and *Uke* sit with their big toes crossed under them and the knees opened. Those who have not tried sitting down in this manner will soon feel pain all over their legs, but within a short time they will be able to sit thus without pain. They must be so balanced that even if pushed lightly on the shoulder, they will not go over backward.

Uke: Grasps both of *Nage's* wrists from the outside, with his thumbs facing upward (Photo 63).

Nage: Though *Uke* holds *Nage's* wrists tightly, *Nage* does not attempt to resist, assumes an immovable posture and with unbending arms pushes his hips forward, and *Uke* falls backward. At this time, if *Nage* stretches his left arm farther, *Uke* will fall to the left side of *Nage* (Photo 64).

Nage follows *Uke's* body as he falls, holds him with *Ki*, and hits *Uke's* face with his right hand (Photo 65).

Photo 63: *Nage* should not think that he is being held by *Uke*. If he does, he will be overwhelmed by *Uke's Ki* and will not be able to pour forth his own *Ki*. He can think that he is allowing *Uke* to hold him or that something has alighted on his arms. Though *Uke* is there, he can be completely ignored, or thought of as thin air. Then he can pour forth his *Ki* through his unbendable arms and with the mental picture of moving a mountain a thousand miles away advance upon *Uke*.

Photo 64: *Nage* should not lift his hips from the floor. If he does, his *Ki* will disappear. He must keep his toes up. If he pushes with mere strength alone, his opponent will not oblige him

by moving. But if he pushes with *Ki*, his opponent falls easily.

When *Nage* tries to throw *Uke* to his left, he usually pulls *Uke's* left hand toward himself. In *AIKIDO*, there is one exercise in pulling *Ki* toward oneself. If *Nage* extends his left arm farther, instead of pulling it toward himself, *Uke* will fall down to the left. Lower your right elbow and try to push with the elbow and not with the fingers.

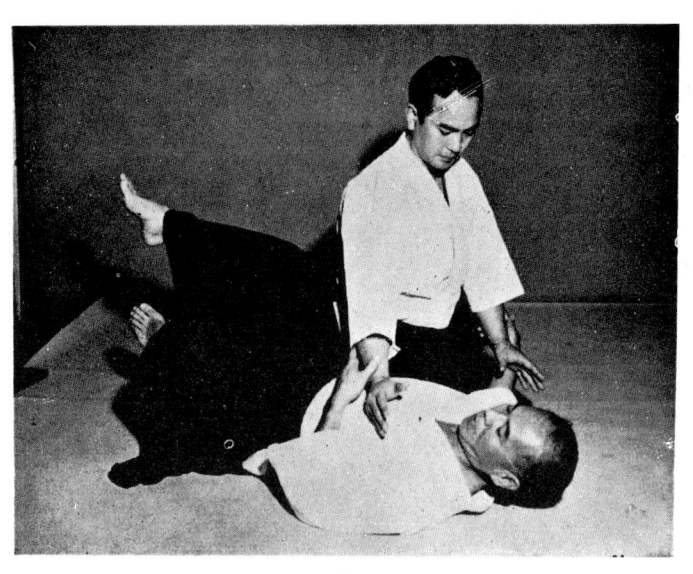

Photo 65: If *Nage* tries to hold *Uke* down by using all his strength. *Uke* can easily upset him. Hold *Ki* to the one point, relax the arms, and let them drop naturally. The thought to keep in mind is that you are not holding down just your opponent but the whole earth itself, at the same time holding your one point stable, and making yourself as immovable as a mighty rock. This is the posture of holding down with *Ki*.

As explained previously, in *AIKIDO* you hold your opponent face down, but the art is not so much to hold him down for the sake of holding him down as it is to do it to train your *Ki*. Therefore, as soon as you have thrown him, you slap him in the face.

No. 6. Katate-Tori Kokyu-Nage

As in Nos. 3 and 4, if *Uke* obliges by grasping *Nage's* right wrist with his right hand, it is easy to apply the correct technique. But if *Uke* grasps *Nage's* left wrist with his right hand, the technique to apply is a bit different. In *AIKIDO*, this is the proper way to hold an opponent. Conversely, if *Uke* uses the hold as in No. 3, *Nage* can use his left arm at all times and attack *Uke*.

Uke: Grasps *Nage's* left wrist with his right hand.

Nage: Immediately extends the back of his hand, bent at the wrist, pours forth *Ki* and allows *Uke* to grasp his wrist (Photo 66). Even if *Nage* tries to pull away his wrist by force, he cannot do so if *Uke* is strong.

It is then that *Nage* can bend his wrist and point his fingers toward himself so that *Uke's Ki*, poured forth along his arm, flows in the same direction as *Nage's*.

Nage's next move is Exercise No. 9. But because his left wrist has been grasped and immobilized, *Nage* does not resist in that direction. Instead, he moves his hips toward the wrist and grasps *Uke's* right wrist with his right hand from the outside and below.

After grasping *Uke's* wrist, *Nage*, without losing momentum from moving his hips, steps out with his left foot toward *Uke's* right rear.

With his right hand, *Nage* stretches *Uke's* hand in the direction it is pointing, and *Uke* releases *Nage's* left hand. Immediately after the left foot steps to *Uke's* right rear, *Nage's* right foot must follow.

With his released left hand, *Nage* grasps *Uke* from behind by the nape of his neck and pushes it in the same direction that *Uke's* hand is thrust. At this moment, *Nage's* face and hips must face the same direction as *Uke's* (Photo 67).

When *Uke* is pushed down and tries to rise up again, *Nage*, while still holding *Uke's* neck with his left hand, wraps his right arm around *Uke's* neck from below, and throws *Uke* backward with the same technique used in No. 3 (Photo 55).

Photo 66: To release his left wrist from *Uke's* right hand, *Nage* must never try to do so by pulling. It simply will not work. The thing for him to do is to bend his wrist fully and pour forth *Ki*, then while he pulls at *Uke's* right arm with his own right arm, *Nage* should leap into *Uke's* side. *Uke's* grasp easily comes off.

Photo 67: No matter how powerful the man may be who grasps your wrist, you are always calm. That is because you do not oppose power with power. Since you do not depend on your opponent's strength, you are not at all excited at his physical strength. In *AIKIDO*, it may appear to one who looks only at the form that two men are struggling with each other, but in *Ki*, there is absolutely no resistance, and the contest becomes essentially an exhibition of non-resistant techniques. Even when *Uke* grasps *Nage* with both hands, there is a non-resistant technique that can be used by *Nage* to subdue him.

No. 7. Katate-Tori Kote-Gaeshi

Nage frees his left hand in the same manner as in technique No. 6, but instead of grasping *Uke* by the neck grasps his left wrist. Then, with his right hand grasping *Uke's* right hand, *Nage* feints by pushing that hand away and changes his hold by releasing the left wrist and grasping *Uke's* right wrist with his left hand.

Nage continues without loss of momentum as though to stretch *Uke's* right arm to make a half-turn to his right. As *Uke* follows *Nage's* lead, *Nage* applies *Kote-Gaeshi* as in Technique No. 4.

68   69

When changing his hold from the right hand to the left, *Nage* must use mainly the little finger and the ring finger. If he puts strength into the thumb and index finger to change hands, he will find that his fingers may slip off.

In *AIKIDO*, when it is necessary to grasp, the little finger and ring finger are mainly used. The reason is simple. If one puts strength into the thumb and index finger, one's strength rises up to the shoulder and becomes separated from the one point and is dissipated.

If one is relaxed and the side of the hand thrust out with strength put into the little finger, strength connects naturally in a continuous flow with the one point.

The mind has rules for the mind; the body has rules for the body.

The rules of the body are to use the body to rectify the rules of the mind. Thus the powers of mind and body can be used in full coordination.

No. 8. Katate-Tori Kokyu-Nage Irimi

Uke: Grasps *Nage*'s left wrist with his right hand.

Nage: Drops the left arm in a very relaxed way, and tries not to receive *Uke*'s power, but keeps the fingers pointing toward his back.

Next he lowers his hips, steps forward with his right foot, then with the left foot to the right side of *Uke*. With the left hand, he leads *Uke*'s right arm to his right rear. He bends his right arm, lowering the elbow and pointing the fingers upward, and keeps the forearm close to *Uke*'s chest (Photo 70).

Then, as *Uke* loses his balance, *Nage* raises his right foot and steps forward to the foot behind *Uke*. He slides his right arm up and wraps it around *Uke*'s neck, pointing the fingers downward (Photo 71). Simultaneously with *Nage*'s placing his right foot behind *Uke*, *Nage* pushes his right arm down as though to drive the fingertips into the ground, and lets *Uke* fall to the mat.

Nage will have plenty of *Ki* in his hips during this movement.

70   71

Photo 70: *Uke* naturally tries to bear down on *Nage* and prevent him from advancing to his side. It will be difficult to step in against this resistance. If *Nage* pushes back *Uke*'s right arm, he will be using force against force. In this case, *Nage* should lead *Uke*'s right arm to the extent of stretching his arm slightly. Then he can move *Uke* no matter how strong he may be.

Therefore, *Nage* must relax, pour forth *Ki* along his left arm, leap in with his hips, move *Uke's* arm like the swinging of a pendulum. It is difficult to move him with the arm alone.

If *Nage's* right forearm were to strike *Uke's* chest, *Uke* will be able to resist him. Instead, before *Uke* realizes that the forearm is close to his chest, it must be slid upward and wrapped around *Uke's* neck.

Nage's intention here is not to throw *Uke's* body down but rather to lead *Uke's* Ki toward the rear. The left hand is always leading *Uke's* arm to the rear so that he will be kept in an unbalanced posture.

When *Nage* follows this procedure, no matter how powerful *Uke* may be, as strong as a wind that blows down a great tree, *Nage* can easily make *Uke* fall.

This is the basic principle of *Irimi*—to leap into the same direction in which the opponent is advancing, not colliding with his strength but leading him.

Again, even if *Uke* may not grasp *Nage's* hand, *Nage* holds *Uke's* right shoulder with his left hand, making *Uke's* shoulder move backward. He wraps his right arm around *Uke's* neck, leaps past him and is able to make *Uke* fall.

This technique is applied at the moment when *Nage* and *Uke* pass by each other.

No. 9. Katate-Tori Kokyu-Nage Tenkan

Without resisting your opponent's strength, but stretching it out and leading it in a circular movement—this is *Tenkan*.

Uke: Grasps *Nage's* left wrist with right hand. *Nage:* Changes position as in

Technique No. 8 (Photo 72). Without losing momentum, he pours forth *Ki* through the fingertips of his left hand, making the one point as the center, and turns to the right. *Nage's* throat must turn and face the direction in which the body moves. The mind also must move in the direction of the body's movement. If the mind remains behind even for an instant, *Uke* will not follow *Nage's* lead.

Nage then chooses the moment when he will lower his hips and his left arm, and waits for *Uke* to catch up (Photo 73). As *Uke* does so, *Nage* raises his hips, slides his left arm, palm up, to *Uke's* neck, and steps in with his left foot to *Uke's* rear, lowers his hips and his left arm again and causes *Uke* to fall backward (Photo 74).

The use of the hips and the left arm in this technique is the same as in Exercise No. 10, *Sayu Undo*.

74

In this technique, if necessary *Nage* can strike *Uke's* chest or abdomen.

Photo 72: It will not do for *Nage* to let his left arm be pulled back by *Uke's* right arm. If he will concentrate on the one point, pour forth *Ki* from the fingertips of his left hand and thrust out the back of his hand, that left hand will be immovable.

If, when turning, *Nage* turns too quickly, the timing will be off and *Uke* will not be able to follow *Nage's* lead.

If the *Ki* that is poured forth from the fingertips of the left hand were turned always as though describing a large circle, *Uke* will follow *Nage's* lead very easily. At this time, if *Nage* looks back, the flow of *Ki* will stop, the timing will be off and *Uke* will not be able to follow *Nage's* lead.

As mind rules body, if *Nage's Ki* moves forward, *Uke's Ki* will follow and naturally *Uke's* body follows too.

When several persons sit together and one of them suddenly turns to look back toward the entrance, the others follow his lead and look back too. For the same reason, if *Nage's Ki* moves forward, *Uke's Ki* moves forward. If *Nage's Ki* stops and looks back, *Uke's Ki* will stop too.

Photo 73: When *Nage* lowers his hips, and does so while keeping his wrist bent and fingertips pointing upward, *Uke* will be sucked into lowering his body too.

Photo 74: If *Nage* tries to throw *Uke*, using only his hands, *Uke* is not likely to oblige him. But it will be easy for *Nage* to do so if he lowers his hips and throws him. Refer to Exercise No. 10.

No. 10. Katate-Tori Kokyu-Nage Tenkan (Katate-Tori Kaiten Nage)

Nage: Continued from Technique No. 9, Photo 72. As he moves his left hand in a large circle, he calmly moves his right arm from his left shoulder to *Uke*'s neck, lowers his hips and his left hand. As soon as *Uke* lowers his neck slightly, *Nage* grasps it with his right hand (Photo 75). The movement of the left hand is the same as in Technique No. 9.

Nage lowers his left arm then leads it high toward *Uke*'s rear in a large circle.

He presses down on *Uke*'s neck as though rubbing it (Photo 76). *Uke* somersaults forward (Photo 77).

Photo 75: It is important to pour forth *Ki* from the left arm, to lower the hips and left hand fully, make a large circle with the left arm and lead with it high to *Uke*'s rear and avoid a collision with *Uke*'s arm and force.

Photo 76: If *Nage* uses force when

his right hand is pressing down on *Uke's* neck, *Uke* can resist and make it difficult for *Nage*.

Nage's move is to rub *Uke's* neck gently as if to lead *Ki* forward, then *Uke* will gladly leap as though obeying *Nage's* mind. The idea is not to throw *Uke* over bodily but to lead his *Ki* forward so that his body follows his *Ki* and *Nage* can easily throw him.

Anyone would prefer to be rubbed down rather than struck down. If he is thrown down, he unconsciously resists. But if he is rubbed down and thrown, he falls before he realizes what is being done to him.

In *AIKIDO,* you throw your opponent without thinking about throwing him. You throw him without thinking in terms of conflict. This is one of the basic characteristics of *AIKIDO*.

No. 11. Kata-Tori Ikkyo (Ikkajo) Irimi

Uke: With his right hand, grasps *Nage's* outfit by the left shoulder (Photo 78).

Nage: Advances with his left foot and hips toward *Uke's* right front, or back toward his own left rear. Simultaneously, he stretches out his right arm to strike *Uke's*

78   79

face. While *Nage's* hips and left foot are advancing, the right foot moves naturally and its toes must face toward *Uke* (Photo 79).

The right hand that strikes *Uke* in the face immediately grasps from the outside the hand that *Uke* has on his shoulder. As *Nage* turns his hips and his shoulders to the right or toward *Uke's* face, *Nage's* right hand twists *Uke's* right wrist. His left hand reaches *Uke's* elbow, at the same time pushing the elbow up, then forward and downward, pushing *Uke* down (Photo 81).

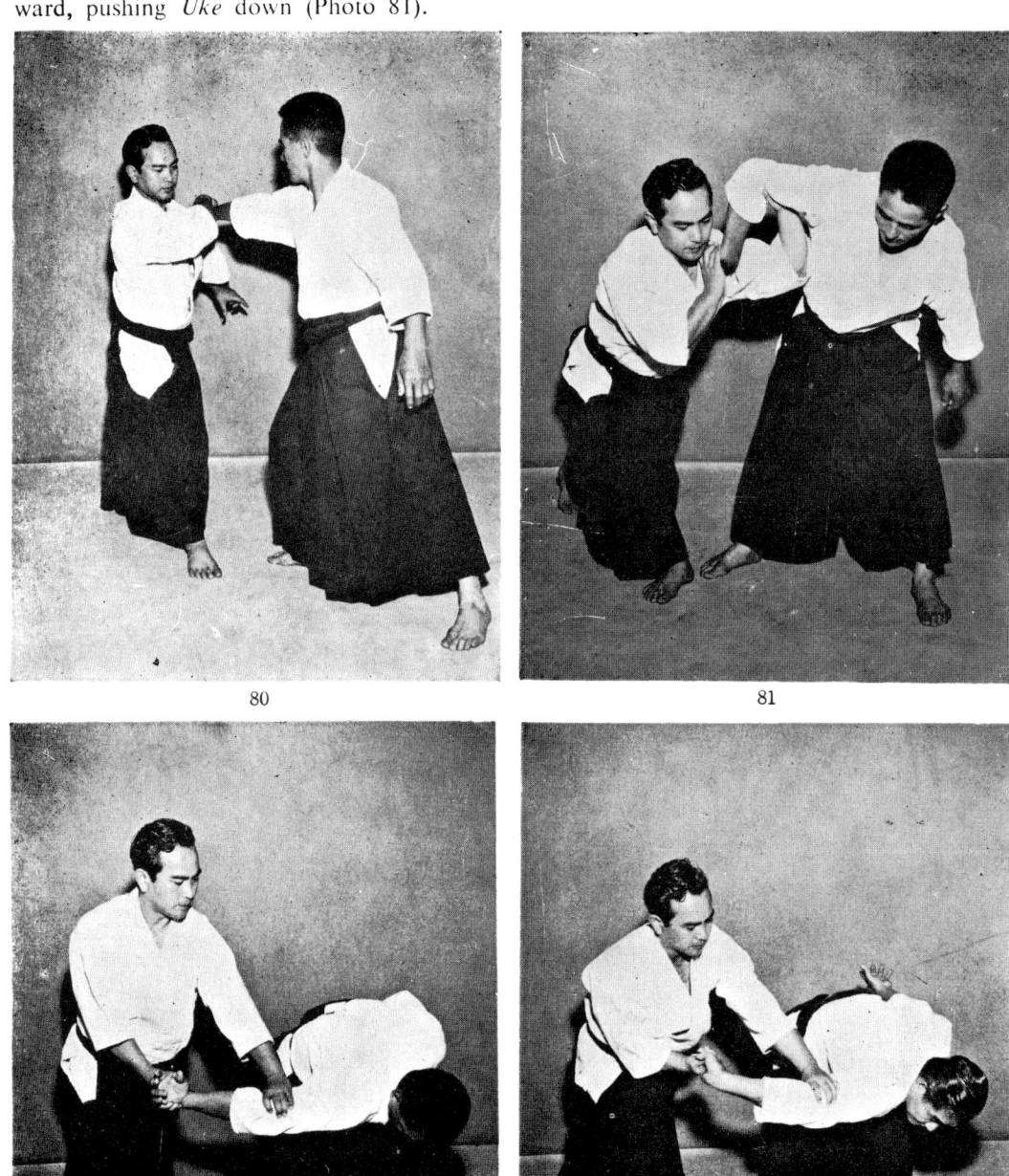

80

81

82

83

In this movement, *Nage* must press *Uke's* arm down until *Nage's* left arm becomes straight and he must keep his shoulder down. Without loss of momentum, *Nage* then pushes *Uke's* arm back and brings him down.

Nage next takes a steps forward to place his left foot before *Uke* and with the feeling of pushing down with his hips rather than with his arms, advances forward (Photo 83).

When *Uke* falls to the mat, *Nage* presses down with both hands on *Uke's* right arm, keeping more than a 90-degree angle between *Uke's* right arm and his body (Photo 84).

At this time, *Nage* presses *Uke's* right arm by the elbow with his left hand and with his right hand bends *Uke's* right wrist fully toward *Uke's* head and forces him to surrender.

In holding *Uke* down, *Nage* does not do so with his arm but with *Ki* as in Technique No. 5, *Kokyu-Dosa*.

Photo 78: Why must *Nage* back toward his left rear?

This is why: As in the diagram, if *Uke* chooses to use his strength fully, it will require a good deal of power to push or pull against his strength. If *Uke* is the stronger of the two, it will be impossible.

But if *Nage* moves *Uke's* fist like a pendulum, he can move *Uke* with one or two fingers no matter how strong *Uke* may be. *Nage* must not grasp *Uke's* hand tightly, but move as though to stretch *Uke's* arm, and he can move *Uke* very easily.

That is why, even though *Uke* grasps his shoulder, *Nage* can move in the direction as mentioned. But if *Nage* moves toward B, *Uke* can attack him with his left arm. *Nage*, therefore, must move toward the outside of *Uke* or else toward A.

If *Nage* moves toward A and leads a little rearward, *Uke* will quickly lose his balance. *Nage's* posture must be firm as in Exercise No. 10, *Sayu Undo*.

Photo 79: To hit *Uke* in the face disturbs *Uke's Ki*. If *Nage* is full of *Ki* he can take off *Uke's Ki* by merely showing his fist suddenly in *Uke's* face and it is not necessary to hit him. *Nage's* right hand hits *Uke's* face and must grab *Uke's* right wrist before the movement of his left hip toward the left rear is concluded.

Photo 81: To bend back *Uke's* wrist is very difficult, especially when *Uke's* wrist is full of *Ki*. For this, *Nage* turns his body and puts *Uke* off balance (Photo 78); hits his face and makes him lose *Ki* (Photo 79); grabs *Uke's* right wrist from the out-

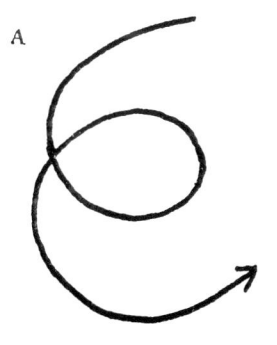

Diagram 8

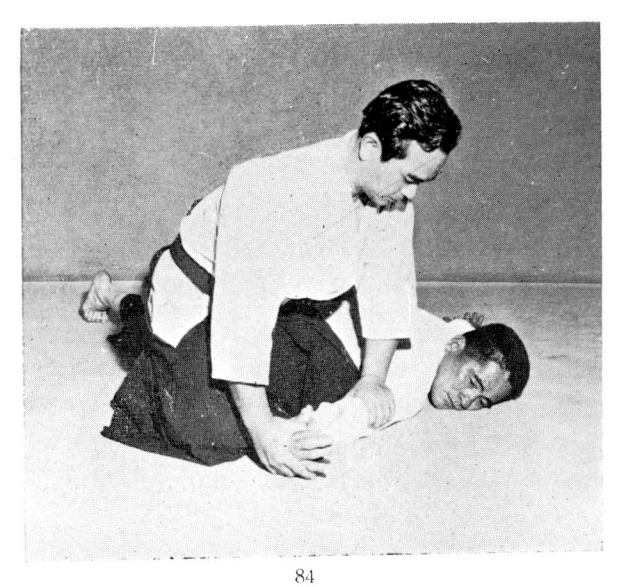

side and bends it back straight toward *Uke*'s face (Photo 80). By these consecutive movements, *Nage* can disturb and push back *Uke*'s *Ki* and gets a chance to push *Uke*'s arm down with his left hand.

Photo 83: It will be very heavy going for *Nage* if he tries to pull *Uke* down with only his arm. But it will be easy for him if he advances his hips. *Uke* easily and naturally falls to the mat.

84

No. 12. Kata-Tori Ikkyo (Ikkajo) Tenkan

In No. 11, when *Nage* is just about to apply the *Irimi* technique, another opponent attacks him from the rear. In No. 12, *Nage* does not advance as in No. 11 but turns his body and can even make *Uke* get hit instead of doing the hitting. This is the *Tenkan* technique.

In *AIKIDO*, *Nage* must change his position constantly in dealing with many opponents at the same time. If he didn't, he would be surrounded by opponents and be unable to move. Because *Nage* turns his body with each movement, he can deal with many opponents at one time or individually. To be able to do so, *Nage* must know how to apply the *Irimi* and *Tenkan* techniques freely.

Nage: Bends back *Uke*'s right wrist and pushes back his right elbow with his left hand. Up to this point, the movements correspond exactly with those of Technique No. 11.

85

If *Nage* then proceeds to throw *Uke* and advance on him, he will be choosing the *Irimi* technique (Photo 85). If he chooses *Kaiten*, he steps with his left foot to a point slightly to the right rear of *Uke*'s right heel. *Nage* leads *Uke*'s right arm, then strikes it down, at the same time turning his body to his own right, and leading

106

Uke's arm in a circular movement and pressing him down (Photo 86).

When this is done, *Uke* will be in *Nage*'s original position and the third person may be the one who will hit *Uke* on the head.

When *Nage* strikes *Uke*'s arm down, *Nage* might easily be led to commit the error of pushing with the left hand and pulling with the right. If the technique is applied in this manner, *Uke* will not fall easily. But if *Nage*, pouring forth *Ki* along both arms, presses down with both arms as he turns, *Uke* automatically falls to the mat.

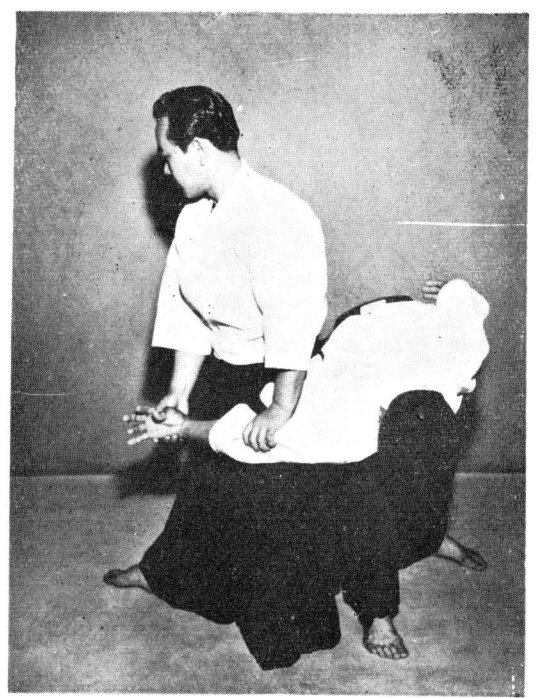

86

No. 13. Kata-Tori Nikyo (Nikajo) Irimi

The movements are exactly the same as in Technique No. 11 up to Photo 81.

Nage: Holding *Uke*'s right forearm with his left hand, pushes tightly with his right hand the back of *Uke*'s right hand to bring it close to his own left shoulder by leading it with both hands. Then *Nage* uses his left hand to lead *Uke*'s arm, grasping it after bending it fully at the wrist. He pushes *Uke*'s right forearm down as though to split his body down the middle (Photo 87). *Uke* cannot stand the pain and sits down but *Nage* then seizes *Uke*'s right elbow again with his left hand and throw him to the mat.

This technique is the same as Exercise No. 1. In exercising, you usually train yourself. But in Technique No. 13, you are trained by your opponent.

Do not push *Uke*'s wrist down suddenly. Because this technique is painful to the one on whom it is applied, it is

87

advisable to apply it very gently to beginners. It can be dangerous for *Uke* if he resists unnecessarily. If the training is taken gradually and the muscles and sinews are stretched and loosened, you not only feel no pain but after the exercises, you naturally feel fine. Do not be over-anxious and try to make your wrist strong overnight.

Because there is some pain involved in *AIKIDO*, many students are inclined to think that it might be harmful to the body. On the contrary, it is good for the health. There is no need to worry at all because the wrist is bent only in the natural way that it bends, the elbows are bent only in the direction they naturally bend. Then sinews are tight when not exercised and become painful when first stretched, but when gradually relaxed, there will be no more stiffened shoulders. One point to remember is that if *Uke* resists unnecessarily, the force that he exerts boomerangs. *Nage* and *Uke* must both so practice as to avoid unnecessary resistance.

No. 14. Kata-Tori Nikyo (Nikajo) Tenkan

Technique No. 14 is a combination of No. 12 and No. 13.

As soon as *Nage* bends *Uke's* wrist, he turns his body toward *Uke's* right rear, holding *Uke's* right wrist with his right hand, and applies the *Nikyo* technique, then pushes *Uke* down as in Technique No. 12.

No. 15. Kata-Tori Kokyu-Nage Irimi

The movements are the same as in Technique No. 8, *Katate-Tori Kokyu-Nage Irimi*.

Uke: Grasps *Nage's* outfit by the left shoulder with his right hand.

88   89

Nage: Grasps *Uke*'s right sleeve gently from below but absolutely does not pull *Uke* toward him. Then at the instant when he has fully poured forth his *Ki, Nage* jerks downward, leading *Uke's Ki* to this spot. It is not necessary for *Nage* to put *Uke* off balance, but only to jerk down suddenly with his left arm as far as the sleeve can go. He then bends his right arm with fingertips pointing upward and prepares to leap in (Photo 88).

Nage turns his hips slightly to the left to avoid receiving the force of *Uke*'s right arm, steps in deep behind *Uke*'s right side with his right foot. The right arm, without striking *Uke*'s chest, slides up and wraps itself around his neck (Photo 89).

As soon as the right foot goes down, *Nage* thrusts his right arm down as though to thrust the fingertips into the ground and *Uke* will fall to the mat.

Photo 88: If *Nage* pull *Uke*'s sleeves toward himself and steps in with his right foot, all the power of *Uke*'s right hand will fall on *Nage* and *Nage* himself will fall.

Instead of this, *Nage* lets *Uke*'s *Ki* stop at his sleeves, turns his hips to let *Uke*'s *Ki* flow away and then steps in with his right foot.

No. 16. Kata-Tori Kokyu-Nage Tenkan

Uke: Approaches *Nage* to grab his left shoulder with his right hand (Photo 90).

Nage: Waits to let *Uke* grab him by the shoulder. When *Uke*'s right hand almost touches it, *Nage* turns his hips to the left, steps with his left foot to the left rear, making *Uke*'s hand miss. *Nage* grasps that hand from below with his left hand, strikes it down with the edge of his right hand, or hits *Uke* on the scruff of his neck (Photo 91).

Uke has not only been made to miss grabbing *Nage*'s shoulder but he has had his right arm stretched and has been struck with *Nage*'s right hand. The direct consequence is that *Uke* will go down in the direction toward which he had been reaching when he tried to grab *Nage* by the shoulder.

Photo 90: It is important for *Nage* to turn his body at the instant that *Uke*'s hand is about to touch him.

When some one wants to sit down and his mind is on the chair he is about to sit on, and that chair is unexpectedly pulled back, he will fall to the floor. If the chair is taken away too soon, he will notice that fact and stop himself in time but if he has set his mind on sitting and the chair is taken away, he cannot stop his action midway, so he takes a tumble.

The same principle applies to this technique. Practice leading the *Ki* in *Uke*'s arm to your shoulder.

Photo 91: *Nage* turns his hips to the left, pulls back his left foot, receives *Uke*'s right wrist with his left hand and strikes *Uke* with his right hand. This technique should be practiced so that it is all performed in a split second.

The foregoing concludes *Kata-Tori* techniques, but the same techniques can be applied to *Mune-Tori, Eri-Tori, Hiji-Tori* and *Ryote-Tori*.

91

92

No. 17. Yokomen-Uchi Shiho-Nage

Uke: Taking one step forward with his right foot, tries to strike *Nage's* Yokomen (side of the face) with his right hand (Photo 93).

Nage: Turns his hips to the left and takes a backward step with his left foot, raises both arms, seizes *Uke's* right wrist with his left hand just as it misses *Nage's* face, moves the right hand toward the left and between them holds *Uke's* right wrist from two sides (Photo 94).

Nage: Then with both hands pushes *Uke's* right wrist (Photo 95), steps with his left foot in the same direction, swinging *Uke's* right arm over his head, then pivots his hips swiftly to the right and changes position by turning his back to *Uke* (Photo 96).

Nage: Generates *Ki* with both arms, extends *Uke's Ki* and forcibly brings *Uke's* right arm down to throw him to the mat.

Photo 93: If *Nage* stands with his right foot forward, he may simply pull his left foot slightly backward as in Photo 94. But because he is standing with his left foot forward, he must turn his hips fully and step back with his left foot. If he tried to meet

93

94

attack by keeping his stance unchanged *Uke's* he would receive *Uke's* full force. *Nage* must change his stance as in Photo 94, and let *Uke's* force flow by.

To start this movement with the left foot forward is more difficult. But in practice, it is always necessary to do it the hard way, because the easier way can be learned at any time.

Photo 95: *Nage* pushes *Uke's* right arm out before him, walks under this arm and steps out with his left foot. He must not go under the arm by pulling his head into his shoulders or bending his knees, but he can do it easily if he does it as though he intended to walk across the front of *Uke*.

Photo 96: As he strikes *Uke's* arm down, *Nage* must not cut off his *Ki* and pull *Uke's* arm toward himself. If he does, it boomerangs on him and hurts *Uke's* arm. *Nage* should always strike *Uke's* hand as if to push outward.

In Photo 95, if *Nage* steps in with his left foot and pivots fully and completely, that should be enough to make *Uke* fall to the mat, without the use of any force.

By the law of dynamics, *Uke's* force is applied in moves as shown in illustration A. *Nage* merely leads his opponent along so that *Uke's* force returns to him completely.

It is important not to slow down the momentum of the action. Slow it down and *Nage* will find the going heavy and *Uke* hard to move.

Jesus Christ taught that if one strikes you on the right cheek, we must turn to him the other also. This is the principle of non-resistance, and shows great love.

In *AIKIDO*, the collision of your opponent's hand on your cheek represents in form a conflict. If your cheek is not there when the hand strikes, you do not receive the blow. Instead, the striker's force returns to him.

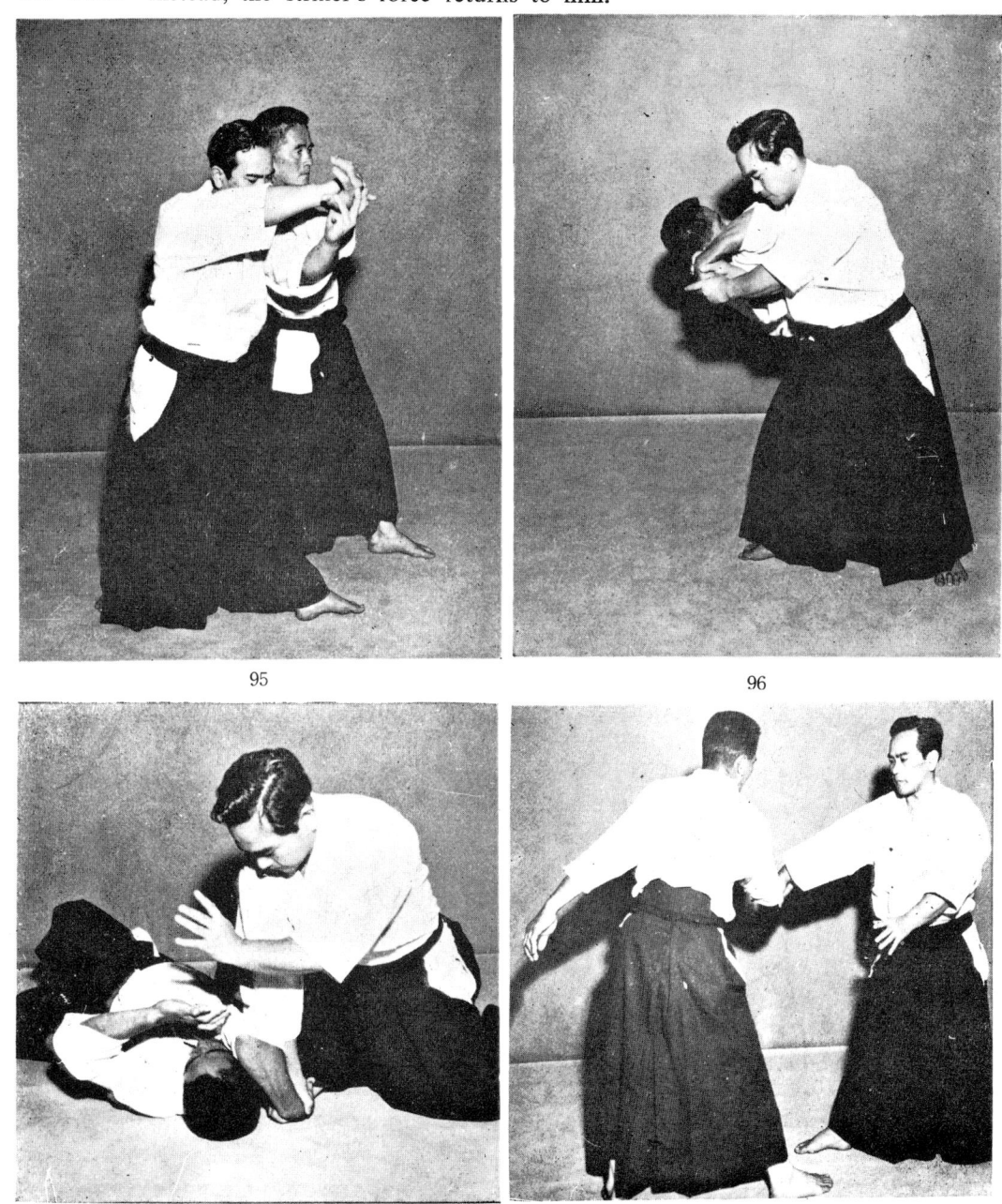

95

96

97

98

If there is injustice in the opponent, let it return to him and let him become aware of it. This is the principle of non-resistance and one of the methods of expressing Great Love. *AIKIDO* and the teachings of Jesus Christ may differ in form but in spirit they are the same.

Photo 94: When pivoting the hips, as in line *c* in the diagram, *Nage* must lead the force of *a* in a large arc. If he were to lead him in a small arc, as in *d*, *Nage* will not only receive the force of *Uke's* right arm but he will come within reach of *Uke's* left hand, something *Nage* must always beware.

When *Nage* leads *Uke's* right arm, *Uke's* left hand must be swinging outward in a circle, obeying the law of centrifugal force.

No. 18. Yokomen-Uchi Kokyu-Nage Tenkan (A)

Uke: As in Technique No. 17, steps forward with the right foot and strikes at the side of *Nage's* face.

Nage: Turns his hips to the left, takes one step backward with his left foot, grasps *Uke's* right wrist with both hands just as the fist almost hits him in the face. These movements are the same as in No. 17 (Photo 98).

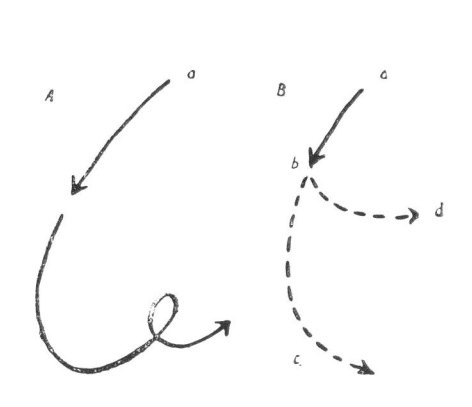

Diagram 9

At this time, without loss of momentum, *Nage* uses his right hand to push off *Uke's* right arm toward his own face, and places his left hand on *Uke's* neck (Photo 99).

After pushing off *Uke's* arm *Nage* wraps his right arm around *Uke's* neck, turns his body completely to the left and throws *Uke* to the mat as though to roll *Uke's* body into his own (Photo 100).

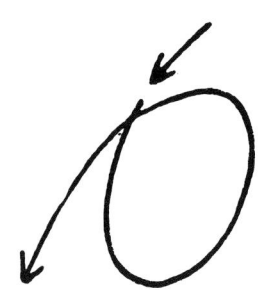

Diagram 10

At this time, the force with which *Uke* attacks must be extended without loss of momentum and *Uke* rolled in, as in diagram 10. You can see that *Uke's* force returns completely to himself.

Nage should not think of throwing *Uke*, but rather of riding with *Uke's* hitting power and making a forceful circular movement, resulting naturally in *Uke's* fall.

If *Nage* stands behind *Uke* at the moment when he is to throw him, *Uke* will not be able to fall. *Nage* remains at all times at *Uke's* right side as he goes around together with him.

No. 19. Yokomen-Uchi Kokyu-Nage Tenkan (B)

Uke strikes at *Nage's* Yokomen. *Nage* takes one step backward and grabs *Uke's* right wrist. Up to this point, the movements are the same as in Technique No. 18.

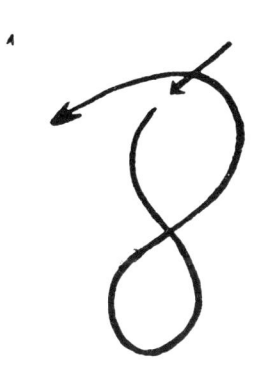

Diagram 11

But this time, instead of pushing *Uke's* right arm back toward his own face, *Nage* stretches it more toward *Uke's* right front and stretches his own left arm toward his back (Photo 101).

Next *Nage* aims his left hand at *Uke's* neck as shown by the arrow, leaps in behind *Uke* and seizes him by the neck (Photo 102).

This leaping-in movement and the following movements to the finish are the same as in Technique No. 3, *Katate-Tori Kokyu-Nage* (Photo 103).

Uke's force moves as in line *a*, diagram 9. This force should be led in a figure 8 and *Uke* thrown without loss of momentum.

All these techniques must be applied always in wider, smoother movements.

No. 20. Yokomen-Uchi Kokyu-Nage Tenkan (C)

As *Uke* strikes at *Nage's* Yokomen, *Nage* takes one step backward and as *Uke's* right hand flies past, grabs *Uke's* wrist. Up to this point, the movements are the same as in Technique No. 19.

In this technique, as *Uke's* force comes as in line *a*, *Nage* stretches the same force in the same direction and throws *Uke* down. At this time, *Nage* may grasp *Uke's* right arm with both hands or may strike down on *Uke's* right forearm or may hit *Uke* in the neck.

At the instant that *Uke's* hand is about to hit his face, *Nage* turns his body, not to stop *Uke's* force but rather to increase his momentum, and throws *Uke* toward *Nage's* left rear as though to make him flow past. At this point, *Nage's* Ki and face should both be toward the left rear.

This technique is the same as in Technique No. 16, *Kata-Tori Kokyu-Nage Tenkan*, and in case of actual attack on a sidewalk, is an easy one to apply.

No. 21. Yokomen-Uchi Kokyu-Nage Irimi (A)

Uke: Takes a step forward with his right foot and strikes at *Nage's Yokomen.*

Nage: Stands *Hidari-Hanmi* (the body turned 45 degrees to the left). At the instant *Uke's* fist is about to touch his face, *Nage* leaps in very close to *Uke's* right side; his left arm pushes away *Uke's* right arm and the right hand touches *Uke's* neck or chest (Photo 104)

It is important that *Nage* leap in so close to *Uke* that his right hand touches his neck or chest. *Nage's* right arm must be kept as is, not stretched unnecessarily.

After leaping in, *Nage* does not miss his chance but with his left hand pushes *Uke's* right arm up, his right hand hits *Uke* in the neck, forcing *Uke* to fall backward to the mat (Photo 105).

Photo 104: *Nage* should not receive *Uke's Ki* If *Nage* pushes his left arm up in the same manner as in Exercise No. 5, *Uke's* force will return toward his back. Needless to say, both of *Nage's* arms must be unbendable.

104

Nage must not merely stretch his arms but must leap in with his right foot and his hips.

It is important in leaping in to do so always with the body turned sideways at a 45-degree angle (*Hidari-Hanmi*). If *Nage* stretches out his right arm with the intention of hitting more quickly, he loses his *Hidari-Hanmi* posture, collides with *Uke's* force, and *Nage's* right arm loses its power to strike down effectively because it is overstretched.

Nage must practice throwing *Uke* with one quick effort, pouring forth *Ki* completely with an explosive "Yei!" at the instant when *Uke's* fist is about to hit him.

105

No. 22. Yokomen-Uchi Kokyu-Nage Irimi (B)

If *Uke* does not fall to the mat when Technique No. 21 is applied, *Nage* should not try to throw him forcibly. If *Uke* does not fall when *Nage* leaps in, *Nage* raises his right arm and holds *Uke's* right arm between his two crossed arms (Photo 106).

Nage then with his right hand strikes *Uke's* right arm down while his left hand has already slid out from under that arm to grasp *Uke* by the neck and simultaneously with the striking down of the right arm pushes *Uke's* neck down toward the same direction that the arm has been hit (Photo 102).

As *Uke* tries hurriedly to stand up, *Nage* wraps his right arm around his neck and throws him backward as in Technique No. 3, *Katate-Tori Kokyu Nage*.

Once *Nage* masters this art, he makes a cross with his arms from the beginning and, at the instant *Uke's* right arm is ready to descend in a blow at *Nage*, uses each arm separately and, without touching *Uke's* arm, pushes *Uke* down as in Photo 102.

106

Because both of *Nage's* arms are full of *Ki*, he leads his opponent with his *Ki*, not with his arms.

If *Nage's Ki* is kept in, *Uke's* right arm will hit *Nage's Yokomen*, so vigilance is needed.

No. 23. Shomen-Uchi Kokyu-Nage Irimi

Uke: With his right hand, strikes at *Nage's* forehead as he simultaneously takes one step forward. It is the same if *Uke* uses a stick or a *bokken* (wooden sword used in Japanese fencing).

Nage: Stands with his left foot forward, gets ready with his right arm to be able to slide up to *Uke's* right arm (Photo 107). At the same time that *Uke* strikes at *Nage*, the latter leaps in and uses his right arm as though to push *Uke's* right arm upward (Photo 108).

Just as *Uke's* right arm is about to reach its target, *Nage* strikes *Uke's* right arm down with his own right arm, steps forward with his left foot to the rear of *Uke*, and holds *Uke's* neck down with his left hand (Photo 109).

Nage's force from both arms joins the force that *Uke* uses to try to strike *Nage* down and the result is that it is *Uke* who hits the mat.

Nage wraps his right arm around *Uke's* neck and throws him down in the manner explained in Technique No. 3, *Katate-Tori Kokyu-Nage*.

Photo 107: *Nage* must pour forth and push his *Ki* forward before he pushes *Uke's* right arm up with his own right arm. *Ki* advances first and then the arm follows.

Photo 108: *Nage's* arm must be unbendable, of course. If he retracts his *Ki* even slightly, *Uke's* entire force will come surging back. If *Nage* pours forth his *Ki*, *Uke's* force is dissipated toward the sides and *Nage* will not feel *Uke's* force on his face. Study and practice these fundamental facts.

Photo 109: The manner of leaping in and consequent movements are the same as in Technique No. 3.

107

108

109

118

No. 24. Shomen-Uchi Kote-Gaeshi

As *Uke* is just about to strike, *Nage* leaps in in the same manner as explained ni Technique No. 23, and strikes *Uke*'s right arm down with his own right arm.

Nage's left hand, instead of holding *Uke*'s neck, rests alongside his own right hand and both hands are used to grasp *Uke*'s right hand from the outside around the wrist, with the thumb at the knuckles (Photo 110).

Nage then turns his hips to the left, bends *Uke*'s wrist and throws him to the mat (Photo 111).

Nage should not be in a hurry to grasp *Uke*'s right hand with his left hand because if he does he will be stopping *Uke*'s force in mid-air and *Uke*'s arm cannot go beyond the surface of the ground no matter how hard it may be struck down. Therefore, if *Nage* grasps *Uke*'s right hand as though he were going to strike it down fully, he will find it easier.

In applying this technique, *Nage* must bend *Uke*'s wrist back in a small circular movemeut as has been explained previously.

110

No. 25. Shomen-Uchi Ikkyo (Ikkajo) Irimi

Uke: Strikes at *Nage*'s face with his right hand.

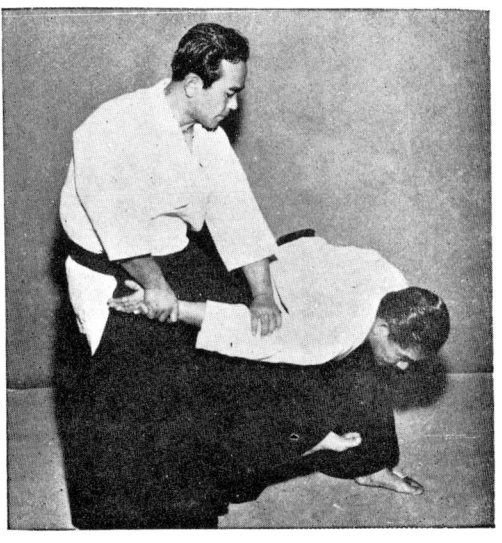

111   112

Nage: Begins as in Exercise No. 5, *Shomen-Uchi Ikkyo,* as though to push *Uke's* right arm up from below. *Nage* pushes *Uke's* right wrist up with his right hand as he pushes *Uke's* right elbow with his left hand toward *Uke's* face (Photo 112).

Nage still remains in the *Migi-Hanmi* (facing 45 degrees to the right) posture.

As he pushes *Uke's* arm up toward his face, *Uke* naturally turns his body to the left, showing his back to *Nage* (Photo 113).

113

114

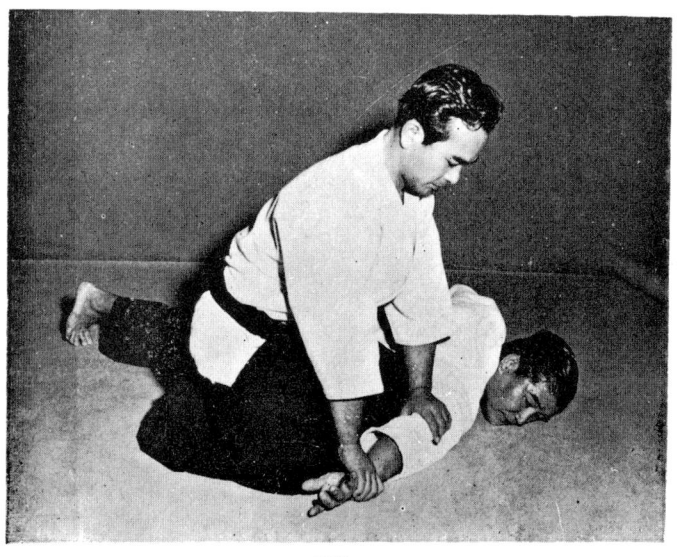

Without losing this chance, *Nage* pushes *Uke's* right arm down with both hands. *Nage* must be sure that his arms are stretched out straight, being especially careful that the left arm is not bent (Photo 114).

Then *Nage* steps with his left foot before *Uke*, pushes him down and holds him down on the mat (Photo 115).

Photo 112: *Nage*, as a matter of course, should be in an immovable posture and his arms unbendable.

115

No. 26. Shomen-Uchi Ikkyo (Ikkajo) Tenkan

Up to Photo 112 in Technique No. 25, the movements are the same.

From then on, *Nage* moves as A does in *Irimi* Technique No. 25; on the other hand, in *Tenkan*, he moves as B does.

In other words, *Nage*, instead of stepping out with his left foot before *Uke*, steps with his left foot to *Uke*'s right rear. As he turns his body to the right, *Nage* also changes position to his right foot, leads *Uke* as in diagram B with both arms and pushes him down.

Nage must be careful not to bend his left arm nor cut his *Ki* when he turns to the right. With both arms stretched out straight, he grasps *Uke*'s right arm and must lead downward if he wishes to throw *Uke* down.

As he turns, *Nage* must face in the direction he is to move, anticipating each move by turning his face. Because *Uke* follows his lead, if *Nage* looks behind him, his *Ki* stops and naturally his timing will be off. *Nage* must move forward so that *Uke*'s *Ki* can follow.

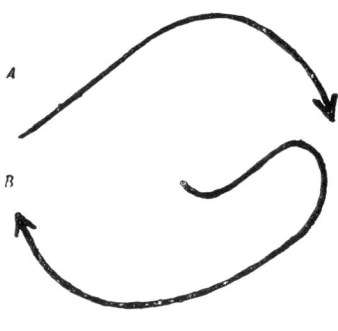

Diagram 12

No. 27. Shomen-Uchi Nikyo (Nikajo) Irimi

To the point where *Nage* strikes *Uke*'s right arm down, the movements are the same as in Photo 113, Technique No. 25, *Shomen-Uchi Ikkyo Irimi*.

Next, as *Nage*'s left hand holds *Uke*'s right arm down tightly, *Nage* changes his right hand to the *Nikyo* hold; with both hands, he brings *Uke*'s right wrist to his own left shoulder, and applies the *Nikyo* art, which is the same as in Technique No. 13, *Kata-Tori Nikyo Irimi*.

No. 28. Shomen-Uchi Nikyo (Nikajo) Tenkan

From Photo 112 in Technique No. 25, *Nage* leaps to *Uke*'s right rear, strikes *Uke*'s right arm down, leads with a circular movement as illustrated here, brings *Uke*'s right wrist to his own left shoulder. *Nage* then changes his right hand to the *Nikyo* hold.

The combined movements of No. 26 and No. 27 become Technique No. 28.

No. 29. Shomen-Uchi Sankyo (Sankajo) Irimi

The movements are the same up to Photo 113 of Technique No. 25.

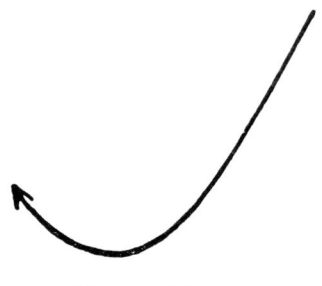

Diagram 13

As *Nage* holds *Uke's* right arm tightly, he slides his right hand toward *Uke's* fingertips, grasps the fingers with the palm facing up, pushes *Uke's* right arm up, bending it like a bow (Photo 116).

When the arm is pushed up and bent, *Nage* grasps *Uke's* right hand with both of his hands—the right grasping the fingers from the palm side, the left hand grasping the back of the hand (Photo 117).

At this time, *Uke's* arm must be in the form of a square. With both hands *Nage* twists *Uke's* right arm and pushes up gently until *Uke* is standing on tiptoe (Photo 118), then *Uke's* arm must be in the form of a square.

With *Uke's* body on tiptoe, *Nage* leads him forward with both hands and throws him down.

Photo 119: When he is about to push *Uke's* force up toward his shoulder, *Nage* must not raise his elbows or shoulders. If *Nage* twists *Uke's* arm as he pushes it up, *Uke's* arm will easily take the form of a square. When *Nage* throws *Uke*, he holds *Uke's* arm as though he were holding a baseball bat and swings forward to make *Uke* somersault as he falls. As *Uke* starts to fly through the air, *Nage* must let go and let *Uke* assume the *Ukemi* posture so that his arm will not be injured.

If *Nage* wishes to take *Uke* away somewhere, he can take the hold in Photo 118 and walk one step ahead, and *Uke* will follow whether he wants to or not. If *Uke* tries to strike *Nage* with his left hand, *Nage* twists *Uke's* arm toward his body. *Uke's* force goes back to himself, and he feels such great pain that he cannot strike at all.

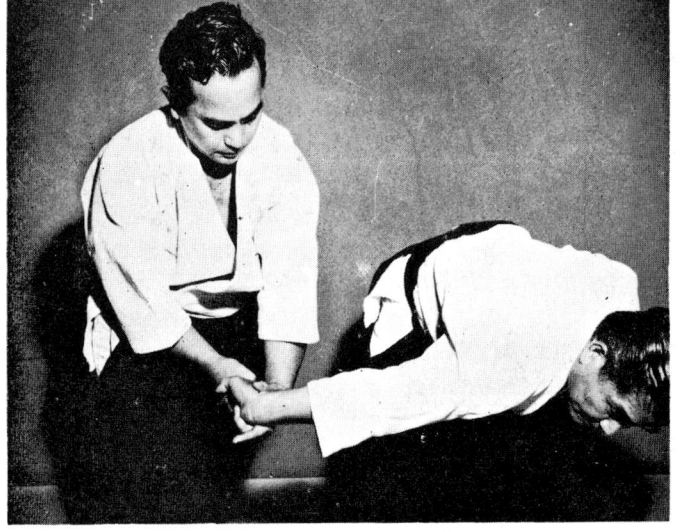

Because the application of this technique can be very painful, it must be practiced gently, not violently.

Even when practiced gently, there is some pain to be borne, but this technique is beneficial for the health as explained in *Nikyo* and *Kote-Gaeshi*. It is painful at the time the technique is applied, but as soon as it is released, the pain disappears and *Uke* will no longer feel the pain. This is one of the characteristics of *AIKIDO*, good proof that *AIKIDO* is practiced according to the laws of Nature.

When pinning down an opponent, do so without hurting him. *Sankyo* is used by policemen as the most effective technique when making an arrest. If *Nage* wishes to hold *Uke* down instead of throwing him, he will pour forth *Ki* in his left arm and strike *Uke's* arm down in a circular motion. While *Uke's* arm is down, *Nage* puts his right hand to *Uke's* right elbow and leads him in the direction in which his finger are pointing. *Uke* is easily led to fall, facing downward.

118

No. 30. Shomen-Uchi Sankyo (Sankajo) Tenkan

As in Technique No. 26, *Nage* leads *Uke's* right arm to his right rear. He slides his right hand to *Uke's* fingers, pushes the arm up and grasps with the left hand in *Sankyo* style.

No. 30 is a combination of No. 26 and No. 29.

119

No. 31. Mune-Tsuki Kote-Gaeshi

Uke: Takes one step forward with his right foot, and throws a punch at *Nage's* chest with his right hand.

Nage: Stands in the *Hidari-Hanmi* (45-degree angle to the left) posture, turns his upper body toward *Uke*, making it easier for *Uke* to punch him, and waits (Photo 119).

At the instant when *Uke's* fist is about to connect with his chest, *Nage* turns his hips to the right, turns his right foot also to the right, and takes one step backward. With his left hand stretched in the direction that *Uke's* punch is aimed, *Nage* grasps *Uke's* right wrist (Photo 120).

Then as shown by the dotted line, *Nage* leads *Uke's* body in a large circular movement, and as *Uke* follows *Nage* applies the *Kote-Gaseshi* technique and throws *Uke* down.

Photo 120: When *Uke* throws the punch, even if *Nage* does not move his feet, he can turn his hips right as to the though to step in toward *Uke*, and make *Uke* miss the punch (Photo 121). On the other hand, *Nage* can punch *Uke* in the abdomen with his left hand (Photo 122).

If *Nage* pulls his *Ki* back, he will be directing *Uke's Ki* to himself and he easily punched. If *Nage* turns his hips calmly he can make *Uke* miss without difficulty. Practice hard to learn this *Kokyu*.

Photo 121: If *Nage* stops the force in *Uke's* right arm, *Uke* can attack *Nage* with his left hand or his feet. But if *Nage* leads in a large circular movement, *Uke's* left arm is made to fly outward by centrifugal force and he cannot attack *Nage*. If *Uke* kicks with his feet as he walks, he himself will lose his balance and fall down and cannot attack at all.

When *Nage* is bending *Uke's* wrist, he should not do so forcibly against the momentum of *Uke's* body, but should move in a large circle first, wait until the momentum of *Uke's* body has spent itself, then bend the wrist in the natural way.

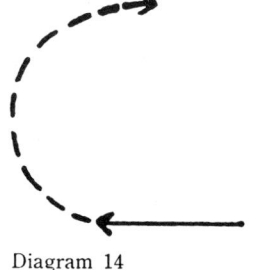

Diagram 14

No. 32. Mune-Tsuki Kaiten-Nage

Uke: As he steps forward with his right foot, *Uke* throws a punch at *Nage's* chest.

Nage: Turns his hips to the right, making *Uke* miss and simultaneously with his left forearm pushes *Uke's* right wrist down with a circular movement. *Nage's* right hand is held in position as though waiting to grasp *Uke's* neck (Photo 123).

As *Nage* holds *Uke's* right wrist and without loss of momentum, leads that wrist up and behind *Uke*, as shown in Photo 124, *Uke's* head is automatically lowered. *Nage* does not miss this chance to grasp *Uke's* neck with his right hand and pushes down as though to rub the head, makes *Uke's* body do a complete turn, using both hands, and throws him forward.

122

Photo 123: When *Nage* leads *Uke's* right arm up and behind him, he can take hold of *Uke's* right wrist in a natural way with his left hand.

123

124

Photo 124: The more *Nage* pushes *Uke*'s right arm down, the lower goes *Uke*'s head and the easier it is to apply this technique. This is the same as Technique No. 10, *Katate-Tori Kaiten-Nage*.

No. 33. Mune-Tsuki Hantai Tenkan

In No. 31 and No. 32, when *Uke* throws a punch at him, *Nage* turns his body toward *Uke*'s right side. But in No. 33, *Nage* may turn his body toward *Uke*'s left side. (Photo 125).

Nage: As in Technique No. 31, *Nage* grasps *Uke*'s right wrist with his right hand. This must be done by leading with a circular movement, as shown by the dotted line in the diagram.

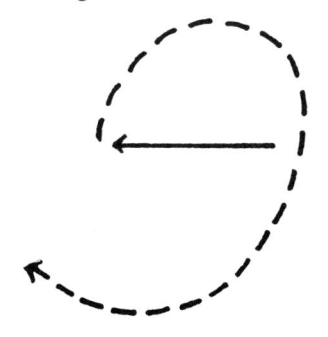

125

Diagram 15

Then as soon as *Nage* has suddenly turned his hips to the right, he brings *Uke*'s right wrist to *Nage*'s shoulder and applies *Nikyo* (Photo 126).

Practice so that you can turn your body freely to the right or to the left at will.

No. 34. Mune-Tsuki Kote-Gaeshi Hantai Tenkan

As in Technique No. 33, *Nage* turns to his left, this time pouring forth *Ki* and just blocking *Uke*'s wrist instead of grasping it.

He follows this up by striking *Uke*'s right wrist down with his right hand, then swiftly turning his body to the left and with his left hand grasping *Uke*'s right wrist.

Next he leads toward the right with a circular movement and applies *Kote-Gaeshi* to throw *Uke* down.

During these movements, *Nage* must be careful to see that each movement leads swiftly to the next without loss of momentum.

So much for *Mune-Tsuki* in its various forms. Whether your opponent throws a punch at your face or some other part of the body, you must be able to apply the *Kote-Gaeshi* technique. The important thing is not so much the stopping of *Uke*'s force but rather allowing him to extend it so that your application of the art will be so much the more effective.

126

No. 35. Katate-Tori Ryote-Mochi Kokyu-Nage Irimi

Uke: Grasps *Nage*'s right wrist with both hands.

Nage: Because the right hand is in *Uke*'s grasp, *Nage* does not try to move it but pours forth *Ki* fully and leaves the hand in *Uke*'s grasp (Photo 127).

128

129

130

Nage takes aim for *Uke's* neck with his left hand (Photo 128). Then using the same movement as in Technique No. 3, *Katate-Tori Kokyu-Nage*, Nage leaps to the rear of *Uke* and grasps *Uke's* neck (Photo 129).

Nage must always stretch his right arm and pour forth his *Ki* or *Uke* will not follow (Photo 130). It is important to move in the same direction in which the arm is stretched. Nage moves his right arm from below in a large circle and wraps it around *Uke's* neck, takes one step to the rear of *Uke* with his right foot and throws him down (Photo 132).

All these movements must be executed exactly as they are done in Technique No. 3. If *Nage* executes his holds and movements properly, it makes no difference whether *Uke* grasps with one hand or two. The result will be the same.

When *Nage* lifts his right hand and turns *Uke's* neck, he must pour forth *Ki* from the edge of his right hand, the fingertips pointed upward and raised simultaneously with the raising of his hips. If *Nage* follows this procedure, everything will be easy (Photo 131).

131

132

If, instead of being grasped with one hand, *Nage* is grasped with both hands by *Uke*. *Nage* is liable to pull back instead of pouring forth his *Ki*, and colliding with *Uke's* force, so that he will be unable to move. Be on the alert.

No. 36. Katate-Tori Ryote-Mochi Kokyu-Nage Tenkan (A)

Uke: Grasps *Nage* by his right wrist with both hands (Photo 133).

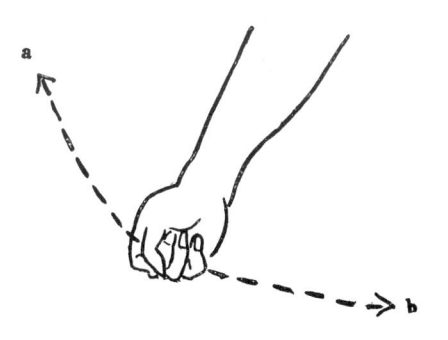

Diagram 16

Nage: The idea is to turn that arm as shown in Photo 134, but when *Nage* tries to do so, he finds it difficult to move the arm. He must pour forth *Ki* through the edge of his hand and point his fingers in the direction indicated by the dotted line, leave the hand in *Uke's* grasp, then bring his hips close to *Uke's* so that his one point and *Uke's* one point are

129

133

134

135

136

close. Then *Nage's* fingertips will move as shown in Photo 134.

As soon as *Nage's* fingers have begun to move, he seizes the opportunity to turn his hips to the right, stay with his left foot to his own left rear, and lead with his right arm as shown in Photo 135.

Nage continues his circular movement as he leads *Uke* naturally with his right arm, and drops that arm with a semi-circular movement, then pushes the right arm up again. *Uke's* body makes one turn and changes direction. This is the moment when *Nage* holds *Uke's* neck down (Photo 136).

Then still continuing the circular movement, *Nage* wraps his arms around *Uke's* neck and throws him (Photo 136).

Movements in the technique are shown in diagram 14 and the momentum must be maintained. Turn always in an immovable posture with an unbendable arm. *Nage's Ki* must always move and lead one step ahead of *Uke* as shown by the line. If *Nage's* mind remains with *Uke* and turns back, his *Ki* is cut off and naturally the momentum is killed. It is like giving a wagon a push from the rear. At first, it is heavy going but once started, the wagon can be pushed with a comparatively weak force. Once it stops, it becomes heavy again. As diagram 14 is drawn in the mind, so must the body turn.

137

138

No. 37. Katate-Tori Ryote-Mochi Kokyu-Nage Tenkan (B)

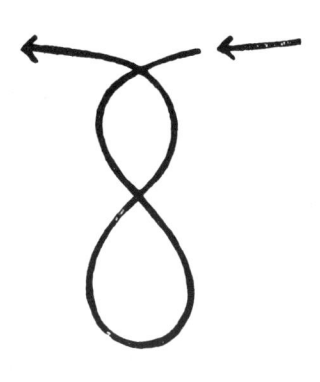

Diagram 17

The movements are the same up to Photo 135 in Technique No. 36. But instead of pressing down on *Uke*'s neck with his left hand as shown in Photo 137 in No. 36, *Nage* stretches the arm fully toward his rear (Photo 138).

From this point on, *Nage*'s movements are exactly the same as the *Irimi* technique in No. 35 until he throws *Uke* to the mat. In other words, *Nage* performs the combined movements of Techniques No. 35 and No. 36 as shown in diagram 15. The movements are exactly the same as in the *Yokomen-Uchi* Technique No. 19.

No. 38. Katate-Tori Ryote-Mochi Kote-Gaeshi

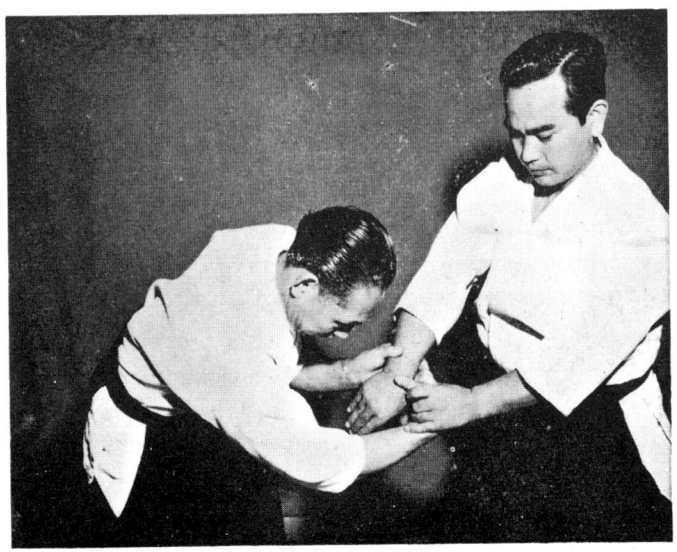

139

The movements are similar up to Photo 135 in No. 36. Then as *Nage* lowers his right arm to lead *Uke*'s, *Nage* grasps *Uke*'s right wrist with his left hand and, without loss of momentum, turns the wrist in a small arc and applies *Kote-Gaeshi* (Photo 139).

When he lowers his right arm, *Nage* will find it easier to do so if he will lower his hips.

No. 39-1. Katate-Tori Ryote-Mochi Nikyo (Nikajo) (A)

In No. 38, when *Nage* lowers his right arm, *Nage* does not apply *Kote-Gaeshi* but rolls *Uke*'s left hand from the outside with his right hand and grasps *Uke*'s right wrist with both hands and *Nage* can apply *Nikyo*. (Photo 140 and 141).

If *Nage* lowers his hips fully, then when the time comes to raise his hips, he takes *Uke*'s left hand in applying *Nikyo*, it comes very easily.

After *Nage* applies *Nikyo*, he must next turn his body and stand always on *Uke*'s left side. If *Nage* stands in front of *Uke*, *Uke* can easily attack him.

If *Nage* holds *Uke*'s right wrist and presses it against his right shoulder and turns his body further to the right, *Uke*'s wrist bends even more and *Nage* will find it easier to apply *Nikyo*.

No. 39-2. Katate-Tori Ryote-Mochi Nikyo (Nikajo) (B)

Nikyo can also be applied to *Uke*'s right wrist instead of to the left.

The movements are similar up to Photo 134 in No. 36. However, as *Nage* makes his circular movement, he presses the fingers of *Uke*'s right hand softly with his left hand to keep them from escaping him (Photo 142), and this time not lowering his right hand but keeping it up, turns his hips quickly toward the opposite direction from the one in which he has been moving. He lets *Uke* hold his right wrist with his right hand and pushes *Uke*'s right arm fully toward the right, and places the fingers of his right hand on *Uke*'s right wrist from the

142

Diagram 18

upper side as though to turn it in a large circle (Photo 143).

He brings down both arms as though to split *Uke* down the middle, still holding *Uke*'s wrist, and *Uke* sits down on the floor (Photo 144). After this *Nage* applies the *Ikkyo* technique.

The movements of *Nage*'s right hand are shown by the line drawing. Momentum must not be slowed or stopped in these movements, as explained previously. It will be desirable to learn to keep time with the hips.

The foregoing concludes *Ryote-Mochi* techniques. Even though *Uke* holds with both hands, if *Nage* keeps his mind only on the one hand he plans to seize, that will do the trick, and he can perform his art as though *Uke* were in fact using only one hand.

Patiently master this art so that you can sense *Uke*'s *Ki* and apply the technique before *Uke* can grasp you securely with both hands.

No. 40. Ushiro Tekubi-Tori Ikkyo

Uke: Grasps both of *Nge'sa* wrists from behind.

Nage: Relaxes both arms and, as though to push the back of his hands down as far as they will go, he bends his wrists (Photo 145). Next, as though to rub both hands against his hips, *Nage* pushes his hands forward, leads *Uke*'s arm out and brings his own hands over his head, palms down.

143

At the same time, without losing balance in the upper part of his body, *Nage* moves his left foot a half step back to *Uke*'s left side (Photo 146).

Then he takes a step with his right foot deeply toward *Uke*'s left rear, lowers his hip, and brings both hands down in a semi-circular movement (Photo 147).

Without loss of momentum, *Nage* rises up to *Uke*'s left rear, puts his right hand on *Uke*'s left elbow and holds *Uke*'s left wrist with his left hand as though to push it up (Photo 148).

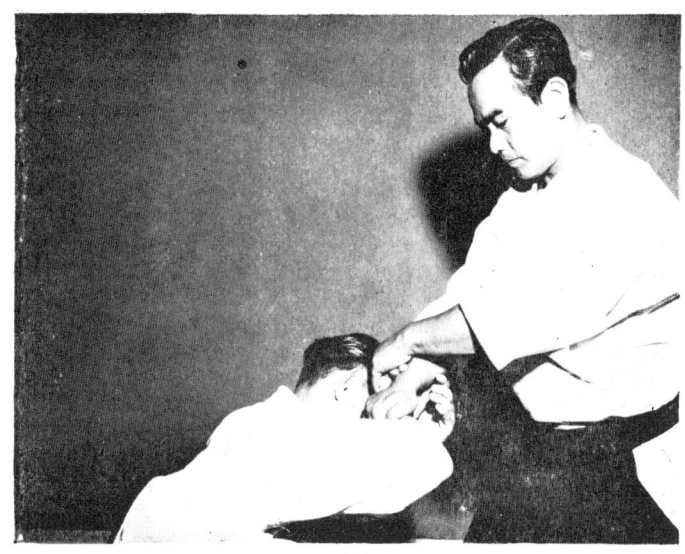

Nage then applies *Ikkyo* and makes *Uke* fall to the mat.

The movements are similar to those of Exercise No. 14. Refer to the test in Exercise No. 13. No matter how powerful *Uke* may be or how tightly he may grasp, *Nage* must be able to apply this technique.

Photo 145: The reason for *Nage*'s pushing out the back of his hand is to lead *Uke*'s force in the same direction as shown in line diagram 17. If *Nage* puts his force into the inside of his arms and tries to move, he will be held back by *Uke*'s force and will not be able to move. *Nage*'s feeling on the back of his hands must be continued from Photo 145 to Photo 147 and the momentum maintained as in the dotted line diagram 17.

Perform this technique with the picture in mind of a huge wave crashing in and then receding.

Photo 148: When *Nage* wishes to grasp and hold *Uke*'s arm, he should never try to pull off by force the hands of *Uke* that are already grasping him. Nage must hold or grasp naturally as he leads in a large, circular movement and rises up.

When a man is attacked from behind, he does not wait until he is securely grasped. If you are the one who is attacked,

146

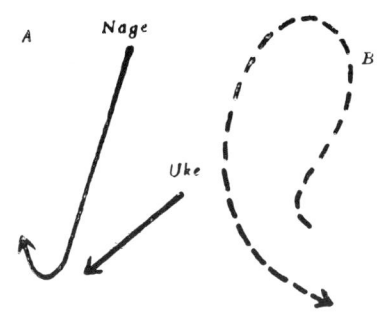

Diagram 19

you must be able to feel your opponent's *Ki* as he approaches from the rear, and turn your body to face him.

When one is not trained to do so, one's mind can face the front but forgets the rear. The mind must be trained so that if a man appears before you, you immediately think of the possibility that there is also another man behind you.

The techniques to be explained hereafter are techniques to deal with an attack from the rear, and training that opens the mind's eye to the rear, and whether one is attacked from front or rear to be able to handle oneself. Train yourself particularly to see with your mind's eye.

No. 41. Ushiro Tekubi-Tori Kote-Gaeshi

The movements are similar up to Photo 146 in Technique No. 40

As *Nage* takes a step backward with his right foot and lowers his hips, he grasps *Uke*'s right wrist with his left hand from the outside and applies the *Kote-Gaeshi* technique.

Nage should never stop *Uke*'s momentum as he grasps *Uke*'s right wrist.

If *Nage* brings both hands down fully, *Uke*'s arm naturally follows his lead and *Nage* must apply the *Kote-Gaeshi* technique so that he will not stop this momentum.

147

No. 42. Ushiro Tekubi-Tori Sankyo

The movements are similar up to Photo 146 in Technique No. 40

However, as *Nage* brings his arms over his head (Photo 146, No. 40) and moves on to Photo 147, No. 40, *Nage* holds *Uke's* left hand in a *Sankyo* hold and swings both arms down. While his right hand holds *Uke's* left hand in a *Sankyo* hold, *Nage* leads *Uke's* left hand in a circular movement and makes *Uke* fall to the mat.

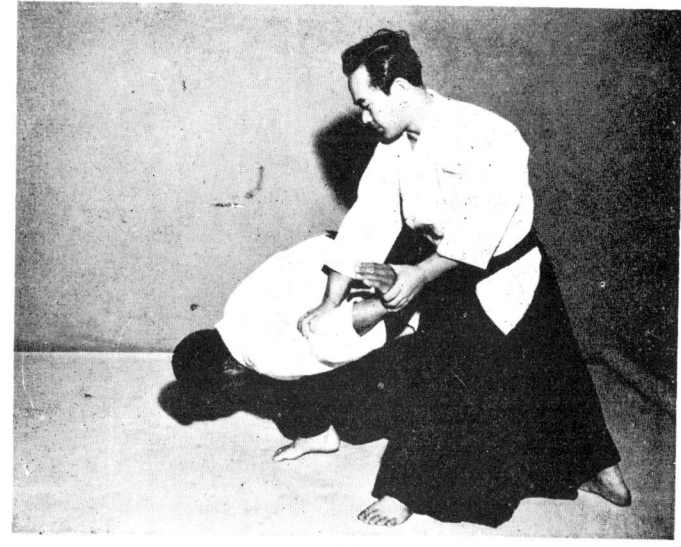

148

No. 43. Ushiro Tekubi-Tori Kote-Gaeshi Tenkan

Uke: Grasps both of *Nage's* wrists from behind, pulls and holds both arms behind *Nage's* hips (Photo 149).

Nage: If both wrists are right beside the hips, *Nage* can pour his *Ki* forward and lead *Uke*. But if both wrists are held behind his hips, *Nage* must pull *Uke's* arms This makes *Uke* draw his *Ki* in.

In *AIKIDO*, *Ki* is always poured outward, not drawn inward.

Nage therefore relaxes both arms, allows *Uke* to continue holding them, and relaxes his fingertips. *Nage* turns his head and bends his upper body slightly forward, takes a big step toward the left front, and turns his hips with vigor to the right, which throws *Uke's* right hand off *Nage's* right hand (Photo 150).

Nage seizes *Uke's* right hand with his left hand, applies *Kote-Gaeshi* together with his

149

right hand and throws *Uke* to the mat (Photo 151).

Without loss of momentum, *Nage* must throw *Uke* in the direction of the arrow in diagram 18.

Photo 149: If *Nage* puts strength into both arms, his strength goes against *Uke*'s force and he himself will not be able to move. It is important for him to relax both arms, to allow *Uke* to hold them, then to bend only the upper body forward and to turn the hips. Imagine the right hand to be a nail and the hips to be a nail puller. If force is applied to the hips, the right hand is easily released from *Uke*'s grasp.

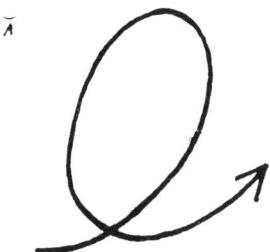

150

Diagram 20

No. 44. Ushiro Hiji-Tori Kote-Gaeshi

Uke: Grasps *Nage* by the elbows from behind (Photo 152).

Nage: Opens his hands fully and pours forth *Ki* outward. As though to turn both arms from the of side to the inside, *Nage* raises his elbows and brings his hands up before him. Both arms will then be in the form of a circle as though *Nage* were holding something round (Photo 153).

Simultaneously, *Nage* takes two steps backward, a small step with his left foot and a big step with his right foot, then lowers his hips. *Nage* lowers his arms and, as he does so, grasps *Uke*'s right wrist with his left hand and applies *Kote-Gaeshi*. The movements are the same as those for Technique No. 41.

Photo 152: If a powerful

151

man grasps *Nage* by his elbows *Nage* feels pain and can hardly move, but if *Nage* remembers always to pour forth *Ki* toward his fingertips and stretch both arms forward and upward (Photo 1), he will not feel *Uke's* force at all. If *Nage* then lifts up his elbows *Uke's* force is pulled upward.

Ikkyo, *Nikyo* and *Sankyo* can also be applied in *Ushiro Hiji-Tori*. Though they are not explained in this connection, they should be studied at this point.

No. 45. Ushiro Kata-Tori Kote-Gaeshi

Uke: Grasps *Nage's* shoulders from behind with both hands.

Nage: Can apply the same technique as in Technique No. 44.

However, if *Nage* tries to move backward against *Uke's* force, he will be held down and find himself unable to move. Instead, he should raise both arms, and draw *Uke's Ki* upward, then quickly lower his body and move backward.

Ikkyo, *Nikyo* and *Sankyo* can be applied in this technique exactly as in Technique No. 44.

152

153

No. 46-1. Ushiro Kata-Tori Kokyu-Nage (Ago-Tsuki-Age)

Uke: Grasps *Nage's* shoulders from behind.

Nage: If he puts strength into his shoulders and tries to twist himself and look behind him, he will find it difficult to do so because *Uke* is holding him securely (Photo 154).

If he loosens both arms, relaxes them and lets his strength drain out of his shoulder, then turns his hips forcefully to the right, the force from *Uke's* right hand slips off the shoulders it is grasping (Photo 155).

Then with the left arm moving in a large circle, *Nage* grasps *Uke's* neck and presses it toward the front, simultaneously taking a step with the left foot toward *Uke's* rear. Up to this moment, *Uke* is still holding *Nage* by the shoulders, and they are in close contact. *Nage* does not feel the effect of *Uke's* power (Photo 156).

In the next instant, *Nage* slips his right hand between *Uke's* two arms up to his chin and pushes his head upward and then downward and makes *Uke* fall over backward (Photo 157).

139

No. 46-2. Ushiro Kata-Tori Kokyu-Nage

Uke: Grasps *Nage's* shoulders from behind.

Nage: In the same manner as in Exercise No. 11, *Ude-Furi Undo*, *Nage* takes one step with his right foot to the right side of *Uke* and stretches both hands (keeping the shoulders loose) and swings them to the left and right (Photo 158).

Next, while taking a step toward *Uke's* rear with his left foot, and swinging both hands to the left, *Nage* swings *Uke* into his strong swinging motion and swings *Uke* behind him (Photo 159).

Photo 158: If *Nage* stops thinking about his two arms but swings smoothly like a pendulum, he can easily move his body even though he has been seized from behind (Photo 159).

Photo 159: Before swinging both arms to the left, *Nage* takes a step with his

left foot toward *Uke's* right rear, avoiding touching *Uke's* body with his left arm and standing close to *Uke's* body, and after this swinging his arms freely to the left and swinging *Uke* off.

While *Nage* is swinging his arms, he can if necessary strike a blow to *Uke's* abdomen with his right arm.

Nage can imagine that *Uke's* body is non-existent and exercise as though he were practicing all by himself.

No 47. Ushiro Kubi-Shime Kokyu-Nage

Uke: Chokes *Nage* from behind.
Nage: If *Nage* raises his chin, calls forth his strength and tries to struggle against *Uke*, he is easily choked.

But if he keeps his *Ki* in the lower part of his chin and does not disturb the one point, *Uke* cannot choke *Nage* in a hurry (Photo 160).

160

161

Nage: As soon as *Uke* wraps his arm around his neck, *Nage* puts both of his hands to that arm. At this time, *Nage* must lower his elbows and hold them close to his body (Photo 161).

As he holds *Uke*'s arm with both hands, he bends his head forward, lowers his hips and makes a bow. *Uke* flies over *Nage*'s head and falls to the mat (Photo 162).

Photo 161: It is very important to keep and hold the elbows close to the body. If the elbows are raised in the struggle with *Uke*'s power, it will be impossible to bend and lower the head as shown in Photo 162.

With both hands, *Nage* must hold *Uke*'s arm tightly close to his body. There should be no struggle in an attempt to take off *Uke*'s arm or to

162

142

pull it down.

If *Nage* holds his opponent's arm close to his body, *Uke* cannot choke him easily. On the other hand, if *Nage* tries to take off *Uke's* arm, *Uke* can choke *Nage*. Be on guard.

Nage must not think of throwing *Uke*, but simply of making a courteous Japanese style bow.

No. 48. Ushiro-Tori Kokyu-Nage

Uke: Hugs *Nage* from behind over his arms.

Nage: To make *Uke's* arms slide off, *Nage* stretches both arms toward the sides and then forward, keeping *Ki* fully running through them, then takes one step forward with his right foot (Photo 163).

Simultaneously with this forward step, *Nage* bends his upper body forward, and stretches his right arm to the front, swings his left arm up and to the rear, and lets *Uke* slide down and forward with force and fall to the mat (Photo 164).

Refer to Exercise No. 12, *Ushiro-Tori Undo*. The movements are similar to this exercise.

Photo 163: If *Nage* puts strength into his arms and especially to his shoulders, he will not be able to budge *Uke's* arms. Not opposing *Uke's* force in the arms with force, but rather as though to lead him, *Nage* can thrust out his arms if he does so as though to slide them from the outside to the inside. *Ki* should be running through *Nage's* arms even before they are pinned from behind. Now with *Nage* thrusting out his arms, *Ki* will be running farther forward and he can easily take a forward step.

Photo 164: If *Nage* carries *Uke* on his hips and tries to throw him, he will receive all of *Uke's* weight and feel every pound of it. All that is needed is for *Nage* to use his two arms and hips to swing *Uke* off. For this, the right leg must be bent fully at the knee.

If *Uke* hugs *Nage* lower about the elbows, *Nage* cannot thrust out his arms because his *Ki* will be blocked and cut off at the elbows.

When this happens, *Nage* reverses his tactics and holds *Uke*'s arms with his hands from the outside and presses *Uke*'s arms against his body to prevent *Uke* from moving away, and sticks out his elbows (Photo 165).

Uke's body comes close to *Nage*'s enabling *Nage* to take a forward step.

So he takes one step forward with his right foot. In this case, because *Uke*'s hips are lower, *Nage* cannot throw him off as in Photo 164. He whips his hips strongly to the left to swing *Uke* off (Photo 166).

165

If, when *Nage* takes one step forward, he turns his hips to the left from the beginning, he will not be able to swing his hips to the left at the crucial moment. For that reason, the hips and the upper body must move straight ahead and must be swung wide strongly at exactly the right time.

When he whips his hips, *Nage* must hold and press *Uke*'s arms tightly against his own body. Otherwise, *Uke*'s arms will be loosened and it becomes more difficult to swing him off.

166

In Photos 163 and 165, it *Nage* keeps thinking about *Uke*, and his mind remains behind, *Nage* cannot advance. His mind must always be projected forward.

Practice hard and repeatedly so that you can open your arms forward automatically without conscious thought, and be able to throw your opponent forward.

No. 49. Ushiro Katate-Tori Kubi-Shime Sankyo (Sankajo) (A)

167

168

Uke: Chokes *Nage* by the neck from behind with his right arm and grasps *Nage's* left wrist with his left hand.

Nage: Holds *Ki* on the underside of his chin to prevent *Uke* from choking him and thrusts out the back of his left hand, bending it at the wrist so that the palm and fingers face toward himself (Photo 167),

As in Exercise No. 9, *Tekubi Kosa Undo*. *Nage* crosses his forearms and with his right hand grasps *Uke's* left hand from the outside, Sankyo style (Photo 168).

Then as in *Joho Kosa Undo*, *Nage* brings both hands up to his forehead, at the same time turning his hips to the right and with his right arm twisting *Uke's* left arm towards his shoulder (Photo 169).

Up to this moment, *Nage's* left wrist is still in the grasp of *Uke's* left hand and *Nage's* left wrist is released for the first

169

time when he twists *Uke*'s left arm with his right arm. *Nage* should not to try free his left wrist forcibly from *Uke*'s hand. He should use the left hand and lead *Uke*'s left hand to *Nage*'s right side. With more experience, *Nage*, using only his left hand, will be able to lead *Uke*'s left hand to the right, even letting him keep his grasp on his left wrist. Then at this point, *Nage* may for the first time grasp *Uke*'s left hand with his right hand in *Sankyo* style.

Photo 168: *Nage* can easily grasp *Uke*'s right hand if he follows Exercise No. 9, but if he tries to oppose *Uke*'s left hand with the force of his own left hand, he finds himself unable to move.

In moving from Photo 167 to Photo 169, the momentum must not be allowed to slow down or stop, and both arms must be full of *Ki* and unbendable.

When *Nage* brings up his left hand, *Uke*'s right hand is unable to choke *Nage* any more and comes off the neck.

No. 50. Ushiro Katate-Tori Kubi-Shime Sankyo (Sankajo) (B)

Uke: With his right hand, chokes *Nage* by the neck and with his left hand grasps *Nage*'s left wrist.

Nage: In Technique No. 49, *Nage* grasps *Uke*'s left hand and throws him down. But in No. 50, *Nage* slips out from *Uke*'s right side.

With his right hand, he presses *Uke*'s right hand tightly against his own body (Photo 170).

170   171

As though to put the weight of his entire body on *Uke*'s right hand, *Nage* does a half leap upward, stretches his left foot to the rear and lowers his body (Photo 171).

Uke's right arm, unable to hold *Nage*'s weight, comes down and there is an empty space between *Uke*'s right arm and body, while *Uke* himself loses his balance and his body leans forward.

Therefore, if *Nage* lowers his body fully with his head bent low and then raises his head and stands straight up, he is already freed from *Nage*'s hold on his arm. At this time, *Nage* must still keep *Uke*'s right hand held tightly against his body. Then he grasps *Uke*'s right hand with his left hand in *Sankyo* style, keeping both hands by his left chest.

Photo 170: It is difficult to pull *Uke*'s right hand down with force alone. But because *Nage* holds and presses *Uke*'s right hand tightly to his body and rests his entire weight on *Uke*'s fist, *Nage* can lower himself. No matter how strong *Uke* may be, he cannot stop this movement and cannot hold *Nage*'s entire weight with his wrist (Photo 172).

Because *Uke*'s wrist is lowered, there is enough empty space for *Nage* to release his head. *Nage*'s head can go straight down and come straight up.

If *Nage* tries to take *Uke*'s right hand away or to pass through to come out behind *Uke*, he will be choked even harder. Heed this word of caution.

At times when the application of Technique No. 49 is difficult, it will be easier to apply No. 50. If No. 50 is difficult, No. 49 will be easier.

This technique can be applied also when someone comes from behind you to grab your hair and pull it back. If you try to take your opponent's hand away, he will pull your hair even harder, giving you more pain. But as you hold your opponent's hand tightly to your head, in the same manner as explained in the foregoing paragraphs, you simply lower your body and then come up again and you can take your opponent's arm in *Sankyo* style.

Because having your hair grabbed is different from having your neck choked, it is better to step backward slightly and then apply the technique. When you stand up, push your head upward. *Uke* will automatically release his hold off your hair because of the pain, and you can apply *Sankyo*.

CONCLUSION

This concludes the explanation of fifty techniques of *AIKIDO*.

Practice each repeatedly; try to understand and grasp the basic principles that underlie these techniques. If you can move your body freely and are able to apply the arts, then there comes to you the ability to create countless new variations of these techniques.

Follow absolutely the natural laws of heaven and earth and do not ever violate them. As water flows into the low places, let it go where it should go; let it seek its proper level; let it remain where it should be, and let it bend where it should bend.

If you know the strength of your own *Ki*, learn also the strength of your opponent's *Ki*. Never oppose your opponent against the direction of his *Ki*, but try to lead it. This is the principle of absolute harmony: not to let your *Ki* clash with that of another. Therefore, both the one who applies the technique and the one on whom it is applied should practice with pleasure, try to help each other to develop stronger *Ki* for mutual advancement.

To be thrown down and have an unpleasant feeling about it indicates that either *Uke* tried to resist force with force or that *Nage* has committed an error somewhere in applying a teeniquch.

Do not throw and think that you are throwing, nor be thrown and think about being thrown. Until both *Nage* and *Uke* can move smoothly as if dancing together, it can hardly be said that you understand fully or that you have perfected your knowledge of *AIKIDO*.

In the foregoing fifty techniques are explained the methods of applying only after you have let your opponent grasp tightly, choke or strike you.

However, real *AIKIDO* techniques are fundamentally applied only at the instant when your opponent's hand is within a hair's breadth of touching or striking you, leading his *Ki* and throwing him, not giving him the advantage or opportunity to strike first and then throwing him or subduing him. Though your opponents may be many in number, you do not let them lay even a finger on your body—this is a manifestation of real and fundamental *AIKIDO* technique.

It is difficult, however, to do such practice from the very beginning. And if you are grasped by your opponent, you will be uneasy and in trouble if you cannot move and cannot apply the right technique. Therefore, in the beginning, practice letting your partner hold you tight, yet follow the principles and apply the techniques properly. Practice the fundamentals one by one and pile experience upon experience until you are able to feel your opponent's *Ki* and apply the correct technique before he can strike. Do not be over-anxious to progress rapidly.

One who wants only to learn a great number of arts and forgets to train himself in basic principles will fail to acquire real *AIKIDO* techniques. He will be like a house built on a weak foundation that will be of no use to anybody.

The fifty techniques explained here deal with cases only where *Uke* attacks and *Nage* stands up and faces his opponent. Therefore these techniques appear superficially at least to be purely defensive. *AIKIDO* believes in the principle of non-aggression, and it is unnecessary to attack. It is enough just to apply the correct techniques whenever an opponent attacks.

Strictly speaking, however, *AIKIDO* is on the offensive and aggressive, because you pour forth and project very powerful *Ki* even before your opponent has had a chance to attack, and apply techniques against him. Outwardly, *AIKIDO* may appear soft and gentle, but *Ki* and the mind within are very aggresive and on the offensive.

Policemen who practice *AIKIDO* in their work are exceptions. They must arrest criminals and cannot wait for the criminals to attack them. On such an occasion, the policeman with strong *Ki* overwhelms the criminal's *Ki*, advances from the side from which the criminal's attention has been distracted. He will make no mistake if he leads the criminal's *Ki* toward another direction as he makes the arrest. If he has had good training in *Ki*, he can judge clearly the direction of the criminal's *Ki*, and he can arrest the criminals before they have a chance to resist.

If he should practice according to the fundamentals, he begins to acquire an understanding of *AIKIDO* almost instinctively.

KATATE-TORI RYOTE-MOCHI
KOKYU-NAGE

SHOMEN-UCHI KOKYU-NAGE

CHAPTER V

AIKIDO AS A WAY TO MAINTAIN HEALTH

Be warned against self-conceit. Know that it is brought on by shallow thinking and cheaply bought compromise with your ideals, although Nature is boundless.

MENTAL CONSIDERATION

1. Exaltation of Life Force

Every living thing in the universe has life force. If you injure the trunk of a tree, you will find that its cambium layer quickly forms new wood and bark to seal the tree effectively from wind and rain.

When an animal is hurt, it licks the wound to cleanse it and speed its healing. When a man is wounded, white blood corpuscles protect him from bacteria entering his body. When a person suffers from stomach trouble, a few days' fast gives his stomach a rest and he will recover naturally.

These are all manifestations of life force. Not even the greatest physician can cure a patient who has already lost his life force. There are instances of patients who have been given up by noted physicians miraculously recovering their health because of their strong life force.

Does this mean then that the most effective method of establishing optimum health is to study ways that make one's life force strong and let it work powerfully for you? We might say in reply that there are many ways of attaining good health—various systems of exercise, diet, sunshine therapy, massage, electrotherapy, mental healing and so on.

Of primary importance, of course, is that all true remedies must follow the laws of the universe, because life force comes from the universe.

Any so-called remedies based on laws contrary to those of the universe will surely injure one's health despite any declarations of its curative powers.

I have mentioned previously that both mind and body were given to us by our Creator. As long as both are functioning, we have life force.

You must understand that you can manifest life force in its highest degree only when there is perfect coordination of body and spirit.

I suppose that everybody has experienced at one time or another the phenomenon of a strong mind controlling the body, and under the condition of perfect coordination of body and spirit a man displaying such strength that cannot be explained by common sense.

For instance, under tense battle condition, you can drink muddy water with impunity. If you did that in your ordinary daily life, you would soon find yourself under a doctor's care. You may catch a cold sometimes even if the weather is only a bit chillier than usual, but while you are under tensions, you will never catch a cold even though you remain out-of-doors all night in extremely cold weather.

This shows that when your body and spirit are coordinated, you can display your life force at its maximum effectiveness and your power will be so great that even drinking muddy water will not bother you.

In Japan, young *AIKIDO* students sometimes practice controlled breathing every night for a week from six to seven thirty. They choose the coldest time in winter, sit on a thin matting out-of-doors, not covering their upper bodies with even a shirt.

Sometimes there will be a snowy night during the week, but they continue to practice breathing, though it becomes white with snow all around them. Bystanders watching the scene with their bodies shaking in their overcoats sometimes catch a cold. But those who sit in the snow and practice breathing seem to be immune.

This is practice in meditation and at the same time practice that lets students experience through their bodies the power that comes from coordination of body and spirit.

In *AIKIDO* you must always study and practice the principle and movement of coordination of body and spirit until you can change the contents of your subconscious mind so that you will be able to display maximum life force.

2. Positive Use of Mind

In *AIKIDO* every one must practice pouring forth *Ki* and never practice pulling *Ki* inward. I have mentioned in *AIKIDO* exercises and arts that just by thinking that one's *Ki* is going to pour out, one becomes strong. When you keep your mind at your one point, your *Ki* is always rushing out, and when you pull your *Ki* inward, you will surely lose your one point.

If you wish to pour forth your *Ki*, you must keep your mind at your one point. These two, to keep your mind on your one point and to pour forth your *Ki*, are one and the same.

To pour forth *Ki* is, in other words, to use your mind positively.

The power and influence of mind over body are very great and you must use your mind always for good: that is to say, positively.

For instance, if some one's body does not feel up to par, he is inclined to become nervous about becoming ill. The state of his mind could so influence the body chemistry that he becomes susceptible to illness. The final outcome: sickness. Needless worry is to be shunned.

Be careful in daily life not to become sick. If unfortunately you do become ill, it is time enough for you to think that you are ill. Do not worry yourself into illness.

If you feel strongly that even though your body suffers from illness, your mind is free from it, you can chase the sickness away, if it is not too serious and even if it is very serious, you will have strong recovery power, if your mind is strong.

Some persons invite trouble, like one who worries that he will die or about what is to be done when he dies. This is an example of using the mind very negatively.

If you worry about things like that, you will feel as though you were really going to die soon. When you have such thoughts, blow them out of your mind instantly.

There is no need to worry about dying while you are still alive. After you actually are dead, there is time enough to recognize leisurely that you are dead.

While you are living, think about life—how to spend every day worthily and how to attain the perfect life so that you can die at any time in a relieved state of mind.

Every human being is like a condemned man from the time of his birth. An appointment with death is made when he is born. Because he does not know the exact hour when he will die, he can live insensible to death. He may be under the illusion that he alone can live forever. That is why when there is some interruption in the even tenor of his ways, there will be much confusion if the condition of his health becomes bad or death is close at hand. Life is precious because always there is the spectre of death hovering near. Instead of an unreasoning fear of death, think how you can make worthwhile use of this precious life so that there shall be no regrets.

In *AIKIDO*, you must believe that you were created from *Ki* of the universe and shall return to *Ki*. Death is exactly like returning home to your old nest. Therefore, crucial though it may be when you face death, you will face it with utter calmness.

Moment by moment, as you follow the laws and principles of the universe and share in its administration, you will be able to enjoy the abundant gifts of the universe with the serene confidence that because you exist as part of the universe, there is not a thing that should disturb your composure.

It can be said, therefore, looking at life from the mental viewpoint, that *AIKIDO* is one of the best ways to keep healthy.

PHYSICAL CONSIDERATION

1. Exercising The Entire Body

No one will object to the definition of a really healthy body as one which is well-balanced both in the vital organs and the bones, sinews and muscles.

It is not a really healthy body if the physical development is unbalanced or the muscular development is good but the stomach is weak.

To have balanced development of your muscles, you must practice the balanced exercises which bring into play muscles in the whole body. The exercise that uses only the right arm tends to develop one half of the body more than the other half. If you use only your arms, the upper portion of your body will develop at the expense of the lower parts. Depending on the exercise, similar unbalanced effects will be seen in the vital organs and sometimes muscles overdeveloped unequally will exert pressure on these organs.

The ideal exercise therefore to keep the body healthy is the one that develops the entire body.

In *AIKIDO*, whenever you practice an art that exercises the right side of your body, you repeat it on the left side so that you become proficient in that art on both sides.

Whether your opponent attacks with his right hand or the left is entirely up to him. You must practice each art on both sides to be able to meet him on his choice of sides.

AIKIDO movements are not only to one side or the other but are ideally suited to development of the whole body, with vertical and sidewise movements, revolutions, turning to left and right, extentions, winding, and all the other movements, using the hands, legs, head and hips, according to the arts and their infinite variations.

AIKIDO movements develop the whole of your body and your inner organs develop equally.

2. Exercises To Make The Body Soft

As *AIKIDO* practice is designed to train one to keep one's mind on the one point and relax the other parts of the body, naturally it makes the body soft and pliable, and the softer one's body becomes, the stronger one will be.

But to relax the body is not so easy for everybody, just as for example it is not easy for any one not used to public speaking to address a large audience. His body becomes stiff and he has difficulty in speaking. Any advice to relax is worse than useless because it only makes him stiffen up more.

Actually if a man can relax his body before the enemy, he already has won eighty per cent of the victory. The fact is that this is the very time when it is the most difficult to relax.

Keep your mind on the one point and you will be able to relax the rest of your body. If you do not know how to keep your one point, relaxing your body becomes a harder task.

In *AIKIDO* everybody studies first how to keep his one point and let the other parts relax and practice how to concentrate powerfully on the one point. The more powerfully he can concentrate on his one point, the softer he can make the rest of his body and the more powerfully he can pour forth his *Ki*.

The relaxation of the body has a direct connection with one's health. No one will feel ill when his body is relaxed, and no one will feel at ease if he always keeps his body tense.

If you can go about your daily tasks with your body always relaxed, you will not tire easily, and you will not dissipate so much of your energy. If, on the contrary, you work always with a tense body, you will soon be tired no matter what you do. There is no question about which is better for the health, to keep one's body fresh and always vigorous or to keep it exhausted.

Everyone agrees that laughter is good for the health and anger is bad. These also are concerned with relaxing. To laugh is to relax the body and to be angry is to make the body tense. No one can laugh when his body and mind are tense, and no one can be angry when his body and mind are relaxed. If you want to enjoy good health, stop being angry and relax your body and laugh much.

Man's body is soft when he is born and all during his infancy. The older he becomes, the stiffer his body becomes, and when his body becomes perfectly stiff, it is the end.

That one's body becomes stiffer means that he approaches the end. On the other hand, the fact that one's body becomes softer means that his body is growing younger.

If you want to live longer, staying young, keeping your body healthy, you must keep your mind young. Furthermore, you must train your body to make it so soft and strong that it can bounce back from an opponent's punch.

3. Avoid Doing Unreasonable Things

There are many *AIKIDO* arts dealing with the joints, like *Shiho Nage, Kote-Gaeshi, Nikyo* and *Sankyo*. We always bend the joints of the body in the direction that they bend naturally and never force our opponents to make unreasonable movements.

Not doing unreasonable things is following the principles of the universe.

If you use *Gyaku Waza*, you may hurt your opponent, because it means bending some joint of your opponent in a direction that it cannot be bent. But to bend the joints of your opponents as they naturally bend and let them move in the direction that he can go are to follow the principles of the universe and not *Gyaku Waza*.

Every art of *AIKIDO* is designed to follow the principles of the universe, and to train and learn it is bound to be very beneficial for the health.

If you practice exercises like *Nikyo* or *Kote-Gaeshi*, you will feel pain at first but if you continue to practice, your wrists become loosened and soft and you will not feel so much pain. If your wrists become soft and strong, they will never get hurt even though you fall to the mat.

Do not be too anxious to made your wrists soft and strong quickly. You must train them gradually according to the conditions of your wrists.

In most sports, you have difficulty adjusting your training to the condition of your body. For example, in training for boat racing, which is a collective movement, you will not be able to adjust your training since all must pull together. In boxing or *Judo*, you may be able to adjust your training to a certain degree, but sometimes you will be forced to overwork by your opponent.

In *AIKIDO*, you can train hard if you want to and you can train moderately if you wish. If you train your *K*i well, even though you practice moderately, you will be able to advance in the same degree as by hard training.

Even an old man or a child or one who is weak can practice *AIKIDO* because it is not necessary to overexert oneself. For an old man or one who is not too strong, it is better to begin with *Aiki Taiso*, and make his body strong by understanding how to train his body and spirit together correctly and by practicing accordingly. In time his body will become strong naturally and he will be able to practice easily even with vigorous young men.

When you feel tired after using some of your muscles or using your brains too much, you will feel better if you practice *AIKIDO* more. It will distribute your fatigue equally over your whole body and let your blood, which is congested in the brains, redistribute itself more equally in your whole body. You will be surprised to discover that you are in better condition the following morning.

KATATE-TORI KOKYU-NAGE

RYOTE-TORI KOKYU-NAGE

CHAPTER VI
AIKIDO AS THE ARTS OF SELF-DEFENSE

Cultivate the calm mind that comes from putting nature into your body. Concentrate your thoughts on the one point.

I have mentioned that *AIKIDO* is the way that teaches you to coordinate body and mind and become one with nature herself. *AIKIDO*, however, is known by the general public as one of the best arts of self-defense. I will, therefore, explain *AIKIDO* in this light.

MENTAL CONSIDERATION

1. The Sixth Sense

There are always innumerable sound waves of various vibrations and intensities mixing with each other in the air. If you turn on the switch of your radio set, you can make some sound waves audible instantly. An efficient receiver can always catch some kind of sound waves.

As sound is made up of sound waves, the mind should be able to produce mind waves and these mind waves may also fill the air around us.

The only reason that we cannot see, hear or feel them is that our receivers, our brains, are not so efficient as a radio set in catching sound waves.

Every animal has the five senses of seeing, hearing, tasting, smelling and touching. If even one of them is lacking, it is inconvenient and the lack may cause unhappiness.

The ability to catch mind waves may be called the sense of mind, in other words, the sixth sense. I have heard that many scholars in occidental countries have begun to study it.

We know that in many ways, the four-footed animals excel man in the keenness of their five senses. Primitive human beings must have had keener senses than we today have. Man organized the collective society of mutual aid according to the advancement of civilization, invented many utensils and tools and gradually reached the stage where it became unnecessary to depend solely upon their five senses for their safety. As a result, these degenerated and became less keen.

I can say the same thing about the sixth sense. I think that many animals have a much better developed sixth sense than men. A horse can read the mind of the rider; a dog can see the evil character of a man; a bird can fly away at just the moment someone wants to shoot it. Undoubtedly man also possessed the sixth sense at one time. If he did, he has almost completely lost it and he can no longer use it.

It is a misfortune if we lack any one of the five senses, but if we can learn to use an additional sense, we may consider ourselves fortunate.

In the arts of self-defense, if you can understand the intentions of your opponent before he attacks, and anticipate his movements and lead him, you will be able to defeat him just as easily as a man with open eyes beats a blind man. You will be one step ahead in preparing to protect yourself from danger before it happens.

If our primitive ancestors had this sixth sense, we should be able to learn to use it again by training. How then can we manifest today the efficiency of the sixth sense?

The answer for this is the coordination of body and spirit.

As one who believes in God with his whole heart and soul sometimes can receive a revelation from God; as one who puts his whole heart and soul into his research sometimes can make a remarkable discovery by inspiration; as one who is a master of fencing can find an enemy ambush; if one always coordinates his body and spirit, his mind will become one with nature and will be able to reveal remarkable efficiency.

Keep your mind calm and coordinate your body and spirit and your mind will be like the clear, calm surface of water which can feel even the gentlest breeze. Conversely, if there are waves on the surface of the water, only a strong wind can be felt. When you keep your mind calm, you will be able to interpret even a slight sign in your surroundings. Once when Professor Uyeshiba, founder of *AIKIDO*, was asleep, several students tried to steal into his bedroom by turns. They thought, "Even Professor Uyeshiba will not be able to do anything to us when he is asleep. Let us test him."

Each time one of them tried to open the door, he heard from within, "Who is there." Each returned, excited but without having done anything.

The next morning they went to the Professor's room to apologize for their rudeness and asked him, "Professor, do you stay awake all night?"

He answered calmly, "No. I had a good night's sleep as I always do."

Yes, he had had a good night's sleep and had been awakened only by the signs that the students had made when they tried to steal into the bedroom.

On another occasion, several roughnecks attacked Professor Uyeshiba suddenly. All were instantly flung to the ground by him. "Before someone attacks me," he explained, "his *Ki* comes to me. If I avoid it and his body follows his *Ki*, I need only to touch him lightly to make him fall to the ground."

Like pulling a chair out from under someone who is going to sit down. If when you attack someone, he does not linger to receive your blow, there is nothing you can do except to fall down by the violence of your own attack.

It is difficult to teach by mouth alone how to sense the intention of your opponent before he does anything and to know how his mind is working. Understanding cannot be given to you; you must learn by your own efforts. You can lead a horse to water but you cannot make him drink.

If you train earnestly to acquire coordination of body and spirit by *AIKIDO* practice, you will be able to gain understanding naturally by yourself.

It is easy enough to use the arts of self-defense when you are ready and prepared. But only by training your *Ki* will you be able to defend yourself from sudden attacks.

2. Immovable Mind

In *AIKIDO* you must practice to keep your mind unshakable on your one point. If your mind in unshakable, you can maintain a strong posture at all times.

Fear of your opponent or anger can cause you to let your mind wander away from your one point. Great strength will avail you nothing if you are afraid of your opponent and pull your *Ki* inward or if your mind becomes frozen and your legs tremble at the sight of a knife or a pistol in his hand.

As you keep your mind at your one point and relax the other parts of your body, you can attain such great courage that you will never know fear though mountains around you come crumbling down around you, and you can keep your muscles soft but agile, ready to move swiftly and freely.

You must realize that if your mind wanders from the one point in a street fight, let us say, your *Ki* will instantly decrease.

"Immovable mind" does not mean that the mind connot move. In fact, if your mind adheres to your one point and can think of nothing else, that would be a big mistake. The immovable mind is one that is not disturbed by what others do or say. As you keep your mind calm at your one point, you need not be disturbed by anything else and you can direct your whole mind to any object you wish, individually and instantaneously. There is a sensing of how to do this correctly that must be developed and cultivated by much practice.

After you attain this sensing to a fairly high degree, you will be able to ward off the attack of not only one man but of many, and your mind will be so keen that you can direct your whole mind to any one individually and instantaneously.

PHYSICAL CONSIDERATION

1. Practice Adapted To Real Fighting

In other sports in which the object of training is chiefly to win a match, there are rules that must be observed; each one must hold his opponent by his lapel or belt; no hitting below the belt; no kicking, biting or gouging, and so on. Without such rules, sports would be dangerous.

This is all right as sports, but if you wish to use what you have learned in training in a real fight, it will sometimes be unprofitable to obey the rules of sport.

The art of self-defense must be one that can be used in a real fight. You need not use the art against someone who hits you in fun. But if your opponent wants to make it a no-holds-barred scrap, it will be he who decides how he should attack you and you cannot call foul at anything he does. You cannot say, "I practiced by holding my opponent's lapels so you must hold mine. Do not kick me, because it is cowardly to do so," or "I learned to fight only by punching so don't choke me by the neck." No matter how he attacks you, you must adapt yourself to meet his attack and subdue him. If you practice according to certain rules, it will become a habit and in a real fight, you will fight according to the rules.

There is an example of a man, master of a sport, who held an attacker by his clothes to throw him to the ground and was himself knifed instead. Without knowing what his opponent is holding in his hand, it is absurd to seize him by his clothes from the front. He should not be surprised to be knifed. His habit at daily practice come out naturally and caused him to act as he did.

Therefore, there must be a differentiation between a sport and any self-defense art. It is difficult to use one art both as a sport and as an art of self-defense, except when there is only one opponent and he is unarmed. When many men attack or when they hold weapons in their hands, the tactics of any sport will be useless against them.

In *AIKIDO*, you practice always to adapt yourself to real fights. You pay attention to the movement of your body, and the *Ma-Ai* between you and your opponent and keeping watch so that you can adapt to his methods of attack whenever he chooses to do so.

Though your opponent is only one, you must prepare in your mind against many opponents around you, so you must keep moving your position whenever you throw a man. If you remain in one place always, you cannot defend yourself from the attack of many men. The arts of *AIKIDO* are designed so that you can change your position each time you throw someone, enabling you to fight many men as they bump into each other, unable to use their combined strength against you.

2. Not To Struggle Againt Your Opponent's Power

In the arts of self-defense, you discover how important it is not to struggle against the power of your opponent: in other words, not to receive his power.

Though you may have strength, if your opponent has greater strength, you will have difficulty beating him.

If you do not struggle against his strength and do not receive the strength that he is projecting, he may be much stronger than you but that means nothing to you.

You may be strong enough to lift 500 pounds but of what use is that strength if you are crushed by a weight of 600 pounds? If you refuse to receive the weight, it could be 500 pounds or 1000 pounds. It is all the same to you.

Not to receive anything means unlimited strength. If you try to stop with your strength a train which is coming toward you, you will be flung aside though you may have very great strength. It is better for you to ride on the train, and when it stops you take one step forward and get off.

Though your opponent may be strong, if you do not struggle against his strength but follow it and when it stops you go one step ahead of him, you will be able to lead him to fall down.

A powerful punch is useless to your opponent if he hits the place from which you have already moved. His power then will only go back to himself.

In *AIKIDO*, you must practice how to avoid fighting and receiving the power of your opponent before you practice to increase your strength: in other words, you should study the non-aggressive mind, following the principles of *AIKIDO* and practicing to get absolute strength instead of relative strength.

This can be accomplished by training your *Ki* thoroughly, learning to read your opponent's before he makes a move, practicing the movements of *Irimi* and *Tenkan*, training your body to move as your will dictates.

3. An Instance of Taking a Pistol Away

I will explain how you can take a pistol away from an opponent as an example of not fighting against his power.

No matter how well trained a body may be, it cannot stand against a gun bullet.

It cannot bounce the bullet off the skin nor deflect a knife blade. It is best not to fight against such odds. If you are not in the path of the bullet, you will not get hurt—that is all there is to it. The only difficulty, however, is to move away from the spot the bullet will pass through at just the right instant.

No one can move his body faster than the speed of a bullet, no matter how well trained he is. Every one thinks that there is no defense against an opponent who has a pistol pointed at you, unless he can be caught off guard. Of course, it is another problem entirely when your opponent intends to shoot you from the very beginning. In this case, you must understand his intention before he shoots and take appropriate action.

Here is a plan of action to follow when you have an opponent pointing a gun at you and ordering you to hold your hands up and threatening to shoot if you move.

He may be telling the truth. A slight move of arm or leg and he might pull the trigger. When you make your slight move, it must put you completely out of range because whatever part of you is in the path of the bullet will be hit.

Only if he is off guard will you be able to move your body aside or hit his pistol down with your hand before he can shoot. If he carefully takes aim at you, he will be able to shoot you in some part of your body before you can move completely out of range.

In the time it takes you to hit his pistol down with your hand, he can shoot you, and though you throw something at him, the speed of the bullet is faster than that. It is more dangerous to surprise him into pulling the trigger by throwing something at him.

In *AIKIDO*, you practice how to move out of the path of a bullet at just the instant you act.

Uke: Stands at a little distance from *Nage*, points his gun at him and prepares to shoot if *Nage* makes a move. *Uke* may hold his gun close to the body of *Nage*, if he chooses to do so.

Nage: Stands in the posture of left *Hanmi*, holds his hands up, but does not put strength into his hands. He must keep his one point and relax his hands (Photo 173).

In one swift motion. *Nage* turns his hips and head to his right and stretches his left hand toward the gun (Photo 174). At this time his body must be sideways from the path of the bullet and must be out of range. If he tries to move father away, his movement will become slow.

Then he grabs *Uke's* hand and gun together by *Kote-Gaeshi*, Technique No. 31, and when he turns his wrist, he takes the gun away and throws his opponent to the ground (Photo 175).

Photo 173: *Nage* must stand in the *Hanmi* posture. The upper body may face toward *Uke*, but his feet must be in the *Hanmi* position.

If *Nage* uses the right *Hanmi*, he must apply the *Nikyo* technique with his right hand by turning his hips to the left. It is also important to relax the hands. If his body is stiff, he will not be able to move his hips quickly.

Photo 174: When *Nage* turns his hips, his body will be just barely out of the bullet's path and the bullet cannot hit him. If *Nage* tries to jump away or to move his legs out of the way, his movement will be slow and *Uke* will be able to shoot some part of *Nage's* body.

The meaning in the turning of his face is that he changes the direction of his mind toward the some direction as that of the path of the bullet. Because he turns his mind, he can move his body quickly. On the other hand, if he tries to take away the pistol, with his face turned toward *Uke's*, he may by mistake help *Uke* to shoot *Nage* himself.

Photo 175: When *Nage* applies *Kote-Gaeshi*, he must always pour forth his *Ki* and turn *Uke's* wrist back toward himself. If *Nage* withdraws his *Ki* inward and turns *Uke's* wrist back toward himself, it will be very dangerous because the muzzle of the gun will point to *Nage*. *Nage* must use the arts so that whenever *Uke* shoots, the bullet will never come toward *Nage* himself.

Now to consider an important matter. When you face the muzzle of a pistol, your mind stops working and you are filled with dismay and your body does not obey your commands. You must practice so that you can remain calm in the confidence that you can take his gun away from him whenever you please.

That he will shoot if you move even slightly means that he will not shoot while you stay still. When you do move, he will confirm with his eyes that you have moved; will report this fact to his brains. The brains will order him to shoot; the order will be transmitted to his fingers; the finger pulls the trigger, and the bullet will come toward you. The speed of the bullet may be swift but it can start out on its way only when the trigger is pulled. Everybody is afraid of a gun because they think only of the speed of the bullet.

If you practice well, it will not be difficult for you to turn your hips slightly in the split second between your move and his trigger pulling.

Since you can take away his pistol whenever it pleases you, you can calmly relax your body so that whenever you do move your body it will be in one swift motion.

When he aims his gun at you from behind, your move will be the same. You turn your face and hips in one motion, move out of the bullet's path and then, turning your body, can use *Kote-Gaeshi*.

When two opponents aim at you with their guns, you can take away one gun first, and the other will not be able to shoot you because you can use the first one as your shield. You can shoot the second man with the first man's gun.

There can be many other situations like those mentioned but if you understand the principles for action well and practice earnestly, you will be able to adapt them and apply the arts and techniques in a natural manner.

SELF-DEFENSE IN ITS DEEPER MEANING

I have described the arts of self-defense which are the arts used to protect oneself.

Now let us discuss self-defense in its deeper meaning which can be called the first principles of *AIKIDO*.

Often in traveling over the boundless sea as a passenger on an ocean liner, we are made to realize how our physical existence is powerless against circumstances.

Or standing on the peak of a high mountain and looking down upon the scenery below, you thought of countless men too small to be seen with the naked eye, injuring each other, trapping each other, making great efforts to protect themselves from each other. How puny are their efforts and how uncertain their existence.

The physical existence of each small individual can never be assured by the effort of himself alone. You are forced to admit that you owe your existence on earth to the protection of nature. So long as nature allows it, you will live but the very second that she decrees your death, you cease to exist.

What if your heart should stop beating while you are asleep? The following morning, you are no longer able to greet yourself in your mirror as you shave.

How fortunate it is for you, even as you sleep at night, oblivious to everything, that there is a benign protecting force over you, that your heart continues regularly pumping away, that in the morning you awake to another glorious day. No thanks in this regard to your own efforts.

You did not protect yourself consciously at night. Nor did you in your daily life while awake. Remember always that you live under the protection of some mysterious force.

This force is nature. Therefore, true self-defense does not stop with defending oneself against others but strives to make oneself worthy of defense by nature herself. It respects the principles of nature. True self-defense must be in consonance with the will of nature. When man observes the principles of nature, he helps to make them the principles of humanity because they are directed toward the good of humanity. True self-defense must be according to the will of God. One who whole-heartedly believes this and practices it will have learned true self-defense.

If you know only a little about the arts of self-defense and brag about that knowledge or use it to feed your vanity, your mind has become separated from the mind of nature and its working is contrary to the principles of sincerity. Though you may master the arts of self-defense, that does not mean that you have a foolproof defense against everything. If your mind is not right, some day you must fail.

Do not think to prevail over your adversary: think rather of prevailing over self. Do your best to do what you should do. In other words, you must train yourself to follow the principles of nature and improve and integrate your personality.

When your mind and your acts become one with nature, then nature will protect you. Fear no enemy; fear only to be separated from the mind of nature. If you are on the right path, nature will protect you, and you need not fear anything. When your enemy wants to attack you while you are asleep, nature will awake you. When an airplane has an accident, you will fortunately not be in that plane.

Trust nature and do not worry. Leave both your mind and body to nature. Do not recognize friend or foe in your mind. In your heart, let there be generosity as large as the sea which accepts both clean and unclean water. Let your mind be as merciful as nature which loves the smallest tree or blade of grass. Let your mind be as merciful as nature which loves the smallest tree or blade of grass. Let your mind be strong with sincerity that can pierce iron and stone. Repay the favors of nature, work for the public good and make yourself a man whom nature is pleased to let live.

This is true self-defense and the chief purpose of training in *AIKIDO*.

The End.

SHOMEN-

KOKYU-

A moment before, these opponents had been holding the author by his hands, neck, waist, etc. Now they are all on the floor.

CHAPTER VII
A SKETCH OF THE AUTHOR'S LIFE

AIKIDO strives truly to understand Nature, to be grateful for her wonderful gifts to us, to make her heart its heart, and to become one with her. This striving for understanding and the practical application of the laws of Nature, expressed in the words Ai and Ki, form the fundamental concept of the art of AIKIDO.

The author was born in January 1920 in Tokyo, Japan. He was very weak and sickly as a child and was always under a doctor's care. By nature, he was very timid.

At the age of 12 he began to study *Judo* and gradually became quite healthy. He entered the preparatory school of Keio University at age 16 and continued to practice *Judo*. He contracted pleurisy by being hit in the chest and from overexertion and withdrew from classes for a year.

His year of life in bed was to affect his whole life. Immature though his thoughts were, he began to wonder about human existence and about the chief end of life. Though he did not get any conclusive answers, he realized that in any event he would have to study and train his spirit and his body.

After he returned to school, he was not satisfied with his previous routine of merely listening to lectures so he read any book of cultural value that he could lay his hands on.

He discovered however that though he could acquire knowledge by reading, it did not stay long with him, and though his knowledge advanced, if he did not put that knowledge to practical use, his anguish of mind would increase.

Then the understanding came to him that to master any subject, he must not only read about it but put what he learned into practice.

He began the study of *Zen* and Breathing practice, giving his whole heart and body to mastering them, and did not hesitate to practice any form of asceticism no matter how difficult it might be. When he suffered from pleurisy, his doctor told him not to indulge in severe physical exercise for the rest of his life. Now as he earnestly practiced *Zen* and Breathing, he had no time to worry about his health. While he continued to practice, his health improved until it was perfect. After two years, the doctor could find no trace of the pleurisy even under X-ray.

He practiced thought concentration on his lower abdomen by *Zen* and Breathing, but it was a very difficult art. While he was seated, the art was easy enough, but when he was exercising, concentration was disturbed.

He went back to his *Judo* practice. He was able to concentrate on his lower abdomen at the beginning of practice sessions and he was in fine fettle, but if he was shaken up by contact with a bigger man, his concentration vanished. Though he was able to concentrate his thoughts in the beginning, he could not beat a bigger, stronger man, so he could not be satisfied with *Judo*.

One day he heard about *AIKIDO* and Professor Morihei Uyeshiba from a senior Judoist, and called on him with the senior's letter of introduction.

Professor Uyeshiba readily gave him a demonstration and showed him some of the arts with his students. Every movement was so smooth that it looked like a Japanese *Odori* (dance). Whenever several big young men attacked him, they were sent flying.

As the author had practiced *Judo* and struggled with only one man at a time, he could not believe that Professor Uyeshiba's arts were genuine and thought that the whole thing was a frame-up.

After the demonstration, Professor Uyeshiba told the author, "Come and attack me at your pleasure." The author took his coat off and rushed at him with all his strength. He remembered attacking him, but the next moment, he found himself lying on the mat and could not remember how he was thrown or what parts of his body the Professor had touched.

The author had confidence in *Judo* at the time because he could throw any fourth rank black belt Judoist at Keio University, but he was absolutely impotent against Professor Uyeshiba. If he could understand what part of his body received power, he might devise a method of standing up against Professor Uyeshiba, but since he could not understand that, he was powerless against him.

He was glad to find at last the way he had been seeking. He asked Professor Uyeshiba for permission to become his student. At that time, it was very difficult to become his student, but fortunately for him, he was allowed to do so.

After that, the author practiced *AIKIDO* with his whole heart and mind, still continuing to practice *Zen* and Breathing, and he finally mastered the art of concentrating his thought on his lower abdomen.

In *AIKIDO*, unless one learns this art, one can be thrown very easily. Concentration on the lower abdomen then is the primary art. Since all *AIKIDO* arts are based on reason, the author could practice them and simultaneously continue the feeling of *Zen* of sitting calmly in the mountains, and he could master many matters one by one that he had understood only in his thinking.

During the Second World War, he was in the army for four years, for a while being in the front lines while the War was being waged deep in China, and while under a hail of bullets, he trained himself in *Ki*, mastering it well so that his mind would not wander even under such conditions.

The War ended, he returned to his home and called on his teacher again, and studied many matters which he mastered under war conditions in the practice of *AIKIDO*, and he understood the basic principles of the use of *Ki*.

In 1952, when the author was thirty-two years of age, Professor Uyeshiba gave him the eighth rank in *AIKIDO*.

In 1953–1954, he introduced *AIKIDO* to Hawaii and remained for a year to teach, and in 1955–1956 he taught for another year.

In four years' time he was promoted to the ninth rank, the highest rank in Aikido. In 1961, he went to Hawaii accompanyining Professor Uyeshiba on Hawaii Aiki Kwai's invitation to take part in the celebration of the completion of Hawaii Aiki Kwaikan. His engagement in the tropical Islands kept him for well over a year. During that time, he extended his travel to even faraway California. At various places in the Pacific Coast State, he gave instructions at many arenas, and returned to Japan in March, 1961. Professor Tohei plans to make his fifth trip overseas in 1964 to do his extension instructions, in response to the many invitations he has already received. He plans, this time, to stretch his travel to New York and other points, using California as his home ground.

The author wrote this book while he was in Hawaii the third time 1957–1958. He is at present the chief instructor at the headquarters of *AIKIDO* in *Tokyo*, Japan.